Keiko's
IKEBANA

A Contemporary Approach
to the Traditional Japanese Art of
Flower Arranging

Keiko Kubo

TUTTLE PUBLISHING
Tokyo • Rutland, Vermont • Singapore

First published in 2006 by Tuttle Publishing
an imprint of Periplus Editions (HK) Ltd.,
with editorial offices at 364 Innovation Drive
North Clarendon, VT 05759

LIBRARY OF CONGRESS CATALOGING-IN-PUBLICATION DATA
Kubo, Keiko, 1962–
    Keiko's ikebana / Keiko Kubo.—1st. ed.
        p. cm.
    ISBN-13: 978-0-8048-3792-7 (hardcover)
    ISBN-10: 0-8048-3792-9 (hardcover)
    1. Flower arrangement, Japanese. I. Title.
SB450.K75 2005
745.92'252—dc22   2004024687

DISTRIBUTED BY

North America, Latin America & Europe
Tuttle Publishing
364 Innovation Drive
North Clarendon, VT 05759-9436
Tel: (802) 773-8930
Fax: (802) 773-6993
info@tuttlepublishing.com
www.tuttlepublishing.com

Japan
Tuttle Publishing
Yaekari Building, 3rd Floor
5-4-12 Osaki
Shinagawa-ku
Tokyo 141 0032
Tel: (03) 5437-0171
Fax: (03) 5437-0755
tuttle-sales@gol.com

Asia Pacific
Berkeley Books Pte. Ltd.
130 Joo Seng Road, #06-01
Singapore 368357
Tel: (65) 6280-1330
Fax: (65) 6280-6290
inquiries@periplus.com.sg
www.periplus.com

First edition
10 09 08 07 06
10 9 8 7 6 5 4 3 2

Printed in Singapore

Acknowledgments

First, I would like to express my appreciation to Jennifer Brown at Tuttle Publishing for giving me this special opportunity.

I would also like to extend my warmest thanks to the people who helped me complete this project, especially: photographer Erich Schrempp, of Schrempp Studio, who took the wonderful photos featured here; Anjeli Flowers, 7643 W. Belmont, Elmwood Park, IL, (708) 452-9004; and Edward Campbell, for his assistance with writing in English and revising my manuscript.

—KEIKO KUBO

A project like *Keiko's Ikebana* requires that the composition and lighting be approached as simply and subtly as possible, allowing the arrangements to stand on the page without distraction. Light is a tool that is most powerful when it's wielded with the gentlest touch. You can't improve on a flower, but you can wrap it in light in such a way that it becomes almost luminous. That's what I set out to do in *Keiko's Ikebana*.

—ERICH SCHREMPP

Contents

Acknowledgments   v

Introduction   1

    About Ikebana   1

    The History of Ikebana   2

    Ikebana Today   5

    Keiko's Approach   7

Chapter 1: Ikebana Basics   9

    Containers   9

    Container Ideas   11

    Ikebana Tools and Materials   13

    Ikebana Techniques   16

    Cutting   18

    Supporting Techniques   22

    Helpful Hints   25

Chapter 2: Design Principles   29

    Line   30

    Volume (Mass and Depth)   34

    Accent   35

    Other Elements of Design   36

    Considering Plant Materials   43

    The Process of Making Ikebana   44

    Moribana Style   45

    Nageire Style   48

Chapter 3: Inspiration   53

    Keiko's Ikebana Gallery   54

Chapter 4: 20 Step-by-Step Arrangements   67

    Natural-Line Arrangement   68

    Curved-Line Arrangement   70

    Vertical-Line Arrangement   72

    Horizontal-Line Arrangement   74

    Geometric-Line Arrangement/Triangular Lines   76

    Manipulated-Line Arrangement   78

    Sequential Vases   80

    Glass Container Arrangement   82

    Using Floral Tubes for the Mechanics   84

    The Basket Container   86

    Pruning Design   88

    Stacking Design   90

    Twisting Design   92

    Shredding Design   94

    Tying Design   96

    Cupped Design   98

    Three Basic Ikebana Techniques   100

    Rolled Design in a Basin   102

    Using Artificial Materials   104

    Floating Flowers in a Basin   106

Glossary   108

Resources   110

Index   116

About the Author   119

The shapes and colors of flowers are naturally beautiful without even arranging them. A single flower in a bud vase, flowers in a garden, or a bunch of flowers thrown together in a vase all make enjoyable arrangements with little effort. So why learn ikebana? Though it takes more time to make ikebana than to simply throw flowers together in a vase, in making ikebana we receive more than just visual pleasure—we also receive the creative pleasure of crafting an arrangement through an interaction with nature. To interact directly with nature, or even to pause and appreciate nature, is something we seldom have the opportunity to do in our busy daily lives. Ikebana allows us to rediscover the beauty of nature and also to experience the personal fulfillment of realizing our own artistic vision.

Each of us possesses artistic creativity, but sometimes it's hidden from us unless we have the opportunity to be in a creative environment. Once the basic skills and techniques have been learned, we can convey our visual sensibility and creativity through ikebana.

About Ikebana

The word ikebana roughly means "bring life to the flowers." After the fresh flowers are cut from the soil (the death of the flowers), they are given new life when they are arranged in a container. Ikebana is also called *kado*, which means "the way of mastering flower arrangement" in Japanese. By "way," we mean the way in which we master the art form. *Sado*, for instance, means "the way of mastering the tea ceremony," and *shodo* means "the way of mastering calligraphy."

Ikebana forms were originally composed of three main lines to symbolize the harmony between heaven, man, and earth. A miniature representation of the universe was created in the small container, with three lines of differing heights (tall, medium, and short), and the placement of these lines used to help structure a three-dimensional form.

Ikebana is an art form derived from a combination of several elements: nature, human creativity, and formal technique. Ikebana requires us to craft the arrangement carefully by observing nature, rather than focusing on speed and efficiency. In the process of making ikebana, we must pay close attention to the natural shapes, textures, and colors of the materials. It also generally employs a minimal use of materials. For this reason, the use of one line, one flower, or one piece of foliage has more meaning than the use of many.

There is a basic distinction between commercial and noncommercial arrangements. Although both types of arrangements ultimately serve as decoration and are meant to please the viewer, they each have a fundamentally different underlying purpose and function. The commercial floral arrangement requires speed because the arrangement must be made in a limited time and also requires someone to deliver it to the customer. It also has to match the customer's need (essentially, the desired materials at the desired cost). Ikebana, however, traditionally belongs to the noncommercial category of floral arrangement. It's created for a specific site rather than for delivery, and its purpose is to give enjoyment to the person making the arrangement as much as to serve any practical function.

Those who wish to learn ikebana usually take ikebana classes and spend three to five years learning the basic techniques, skills, and form. Those who have truly mastered ikebana, however, have continually refined their expertise over many years, if not over most of their lives.

The History of Ikebana

Ikebana is a traditional Japanese art form with a long history, although the influence of religious function, developments in Japanese architecture and cultural activities, and our changing lifestyles have also caused the art to evolve over time. At the beginning of its history, ikebana was practiced mainly by monks and the aristocracy. The Rokkakudo Temple in Kyoto is recognized as the original location where monks first began to practice ikebana.

The earliest practice associated with the origins of ikebana centered on the offering of flowers to Buddha at the temple. This type of floral arrangement came to Japan with the introduction of Buddhism to the country in the sixth century. The custom of offering flowers to Buddha is still seen in many Japanese homes that have a Buddhist altar. A few different types of flowers will be simply arranged in a tall vase and placed before the altar in the home. Often these arrangements are made by family members who don't have formal ikebana training. Although offering flowers to Buddha was the origin of Ikebana, it is around the fifteenth century that this practice first developed into a genuine art form.

The frequently prominent display of ikebana in the *tokonoma*, or alcove, found in the traditional Japanese home was important in elevating its status. The tokonoma, an element of the Shoin architectural style, is a recessed area used to display art objects and a central feature of the interior design. The room with the tokonoma was considered the most important place in the house and was used primarily to entertain distinguished guests and for special occasions. The tokonoma in the traditional Japanese home was adapted from the design seen in the homes of the aristocracy, but was simplified to accommodate the smaller dwelling size of the commoner.

It was after ikebana began to be displayed in the tokonoma in the homes of the aristocracy that its purpose changed from a religious function to the decoration of the home. The ikebana would be displayed alongside valuable artworks and a hanging scroll, and there had to be harmony among the items on display. Thus, the design of the ikebana displayed in the tokonoma became important. Just as the other artworks in the tokonoma would be replaced to reflect the changing seasons, the ikebana would also be changed to incorporate seasonal flowers. Even though it served a decorative function, the ikebana itself came to be appreciated as artwork.

In the sixteenth century a style called *rikka* (standing flowers) was introduced. This sophisticated style, created by Buddhist monks, utilized materials that were arranged in an asymmetrical form and placed upright in a tall bronze vase. The rikka style also depicted a miniature representation of the universe as symbolized by nature. Plants were used as symbols to represent the natural landscape.

Moribana-style arrangement

Another important Ikebana style originated around the same time that was strongly influenced by the tea ceremony as formally established in this period. Simple and natural ikebana arrangements were displayed in the tearoom where the ceremony was held. This style of ikebana is called *chabana*, meaning "tea flower," and the composition uses relatively few materials. It is fairly natural looking and is typically displayed in a tall vase with a narrow mouth.

The development of chabana is closely associated with the *nageire* style, which literally means to "throw into." It similarly utilizes an upright vase and is still practiced today as one of the main ikebana styles. Many of the step-by-step arrangements and techniques that appear in the following pages are based upon the nageire style.

By the late nineteenth century, Westernization had not only affected Japanese society but also its art and culture. The moribana style was created around this time and often used imported flowers, following the opening of the door to the West during the same period. *Moribana*, which means "stacked-up flowers," typically involves using a shallow container with a kenzan (also called the English needle-point holder or a frog) inside to support the materials. Unlike the nageire style of arrangement, the water's surface becomes one of the design elements in the moribana style because the container is so shallow and wide open.

Nageire-style arrangement

When the piled-up style of moribana was invented, it was an innovative departure from the standing (upright) style of ikebana used for so long. Moribana is likewise still practiced today as one of the main ikebana styles. Many of the step-by-step arrangements and techniques that follow are alternately based upon the moribana style.

In the twentieth century ikebana became more internationally known. The styles of arrangements were influenced by the modern culture, architectural styles, and art forms, as well as by changes to daily life.

Ikebana Today

Today, various styles and methods of ikebana are taught at different schools in Japan, many of which have their own approach to design. Some styles are quite classical, and others are contemporary to the point of being avant-garde. Just as the traditional Japanese architectural style had a strong influence on the development of ikebana, the contemporary architectural style is a strong influence on today's designs. We find a variety of ikebana styles well suited to the use of space in contemporary architecture.

Natural-looking ikebana was customarily thought appropriate for use with the traditional Japanese architecture constructed mainly of wood and paper. However, both container choices and ikebana styles have changed to match contemporary architecture that is often constructed primarily out of industrial materials such as steel, glass, and concrete. Modern-looking glass or metal containers and sharp, geometric lines generally match favorably with this type of space. However, I think that a blending of contemporary and classic designs can lead to interesting results. For instance, a modern-looking container can go quite well with a natural-looking arrangement, depending on how it's created and the site of display.

The changing lifestyles and developments in architecture have also influenced the placement of ikebana in the home. As mentioned previously, ikebana is traditionally placed in a tokonoma. In the modern era, Japanese people live in one of three primary types of home: traditional Japanese style, Western style, or an in-between type that includes elements of both Japanese and Western design. Ikebana styles developed that likewise incorporated both Japanese and Western design principles, and today, in homes without the traditional tokonoma, the style of ikebana has been altered for placement in an entrance hall, living room, or elsewhere.

In the traditional tokonoma, the ikebana is arranged facing towards the viewer. Other artworks (such as scrolls or ceramics) are usually displayed alongside the ikebana, meaning that the arrangement's size is limited, and achieving harmony between the ikebana and other artworks becomes important.

This is an example of my freestyle approach to ikebana. My emphasis on lines in the design, minimal use of materials, and simplicity are related to the ikebana aesthetic. The freestyle ikebana form is an individual creative expression using natural materials as the medium.

For ikebana placed in an entrance hall, on a living-room table, or in another typical display site in Western homes, the arrangement's size should vary depending upon the size of the space and the anticipated perspective of the viewer. For example, for display in an entrance hall, where space is limited, a small arrangement can be made using fewer materials. Similarly, if the ikebana will be displayed on a table, it can be designed using a shallow container and shorter materials so that persons seated around the table can better view the arrangement.

Arrangement sizes can vary widely depending on the display site, and range from a small size for the home to a larger size for the temple or a much larger size often seen as decoration for a special occasion, such as a ceremony or party. The function of ikebana also varies, from its use in ceremonies to its display in a private or commercial space or its presentation in a public space such as at an ikebana exhibition.

Keiko's Approach

Just as new innovations in ikebana style have arisen throughout this art form's history, a contemporary style of ikebana is developing that is part of the twenty-first century. Today, we find flower arrangements that are a blend of ikebana and Western floral art. East meets West in many ways in our modern society; they have influenced one another, and so we find a fusion of the two cultures—in art, music, architecture, cooking, and fashion—in our everyday lives. In this type of cultural environment, I am very interested in making ikebana that doesn't fit into one rigid category or style.

The method that I use is simple and is based on a freestyle approach that utilizes basic ikebana techniques, but that is also influenced by Western-style floral design and my background in fine arts. It can be made by anyone interested in creating a three-dimensional sculptural form using natural materials as a medium of expression. Since each arrangement is a unique personal statement, the results will vary among individuals—even if they use the same materials.

The materials that I use emphasize a minimalist approach (minimal quantities of flowers, branches, and foliage) that is part of the ikebana aesthetic. My style of ikebana is uncomplicated, but the resulting arrangement conveys a strong sense of identity in the space where it's displayed.

Ikebana offers the reward of working closely with nature, which leads me to contemplate the natural cycle in which flowers, trees, and all living things coexist (nature's cycle of death and renewal with the passage of time). I like to create ikebana to express my self-identity, to present the beauty of nature, and most importantly to complement the times in which we live and the spaces we live in. Working with flowers gives me a sense of connection with the natural world and also a feeling of comfort and healing that comes from the power of nature.

I truly wish to share the exhilaration of creating freestyle ikebana and to inspire others to try and create their own ikebana designs. The following material contains some basic techniques, tips, and other information to help you begin crafting your own arrangements. Each step-by-step arrangement was created using a different primary technique and design style. I hope this provides enough ideas and information to get you started making ikebana!

Ikebana Basics

P rior to starting any artistic endeavor, you must become familiar with the tools and
materials essential to your work. Learning proper technique is also important
because the techniques are what convert your ideas into tangible form. In this chapter, I'll discuss all the basics: from the containers, tools, materials, and techniques, to
the fundamental idea behind each arrangement. Once you become familiar with the
basics, you'll be much better equipped to create your own ikebana arrangements.

Containers

There are two basic types of containers ordinarily used for ikebana arrangements— the vase style
(upright) for nageire and the basin style (shallow) for moribana. It's important to select the shape
and color of the container carefully, since it often provides the basis for your choice of materials and
will largely determine the shape of the ikebana form.

For those just starting to learn ikebana or who have not worked with flowers, I recommend
beginning by obtaining one each of the following container types: a vase, a basin type, a glass
type, and a basket. They all require different techniques to support the flowers inside, but you can
enjoy so many different arrangements using only these few containers.

Personally, I like to use containers with a simple design that will help highlight the natural materials and that can be matched with a variety of materials. I sometimes have a hard
time finding the basin-type container in the United States. So instead I will use a large, shallow bowl or a large dish as a substitute for the basin style of arrangement. I also like using
glass containers, not only in the summertime, but also during other seasons. Because the
glass is neutral and transparent, the design of the arrangement can extend into, and be
viewed through, the container.

In order to select the right container for your arrangement, consider the following points:

■ The size relationship between the container and the site of display: The size of the container must correspond with the size of the display site. Too large or too tall of an arrangement for the small space can simply overwhelm the space. Too small of an arrangement in a big empty space will likewise diminish the quality of the arrangement.

■ The color harmony between the container, the site, and the flowers: It is generally easier if you first choose the site and a container color that matches the site, and choose the materials last, because it is often more difficult to find a proper container than it is to find materials suitable for the container and site. The choice of color is, obviously, a matter of your personal taste; however, keep in mind that the choice of color combination will fundamentally influence the overall appearance of your arrangement. For example, the use of monochromatic color (using lighter and darker colors from the same color group) creates a calm feeling. In contrast, the use of complementary colors (for example, red and green or yellow and violet) produces a much more vivid impression.

■ The occasion: Is the arrangement for a seasonal occasion or a special day? A basket or glass container can often be used in summertime, for instance, or a dark yellow, orange, or brown ceramic container can be well suited for the fall. Pastel colors, of course, are traditionally associated with springtime and Easter.

■ The surroundings: Consider nearby paintings or furniture or the wall color where your ikebana will be displayed. You want to create harmony between the container and the surrounding space. Much as you choose paintings and other decorations to match with your interior design, select a container that matches your surroundings to ensure that the ikebana blends nicely with the site.

Container Ideas

Many everyday objects can be used as alternative containers for your arrangements. If necessary, try adding a small bottle or plastic liner inside the object to prevent water from leaking.

The following arrangements are examples of how I have used alternative containers. I created these arrangements with plant materials left over from larger arrangements.

These are some of the types of items I sometimes use as a substitute for the traditional ikebana container: a teapot, some small coffee cups, a tray, and some Japanese teacups

The Green Tea Pot

I like the round shape and earth green color of this teapot. The handmade craftsmanship also gives a warm impression. Only two simple materials are used for this small arrangement: Galax leaves are rolled into a cone shape with some Craspedia placed inside. The yellow of the Craspedia creates the accent against the green pot.

Coffee Cups

Depending on the size of your container and the available space, you can use either one container or a combination of several containers. When using a group of containers, I select those that have a sequential design or color. In this arrangement, I use the line (steel grass) to connect two coffee cups and also use the color for effect (the reverse color in two cups). In one cup, the small pink flowers (Aster Matsumoto) are arranged outside, and I use one green chrysanthemum in the center. In the other cup, I reverse the color scheme—the green chrysanthemums are arranged outside and one Aster Matsumoto is used in the center.

Japanese Cups

In this arrangement, the same flowers (Aster Matsumoto) in different colors (pink and violet) are used to show harmony between the two cups. I selected these colors to match the Japanese alphabet design on the cups. The yellow flowers (Craspedia) are used to create the geometric lines.

Japanese Tray

Flowers, foliage, and some small stones are arranged together in this Japanese lacquer tray used as the container. Because the height is low and flat, this type of arrangement is suitable as a table decoration.

Other Containers

Finally, don't hesitate to look to some of the everyday objects in your own home as potential ikebana containers. You can create unique arrangements that express your individual style by putting a little extra thought into your container ideas.

Ikebana Tools and Materials

Ikebana has its own tools that you should become familiar with. The scissors and the kenzan are the main ikebana tools, but there are others that can help to create the form of the arrangement more efficiently. Additionally, I sometimes use some of the basic tools that are used for Western-style arrangements. As long as the tool helps to construct the form, it doesn't matter how it is ordinarily used. Western tools can be useful for making ikebana, and ikebana tools can be useful for making Western-style arrangements.

Ikebana Scissors

Ikebana scissors cut both branches and the stems of flowers well and are obviously suitable for the ikebana technique. You can also use other types of flower-cutting scissors if you find them more comfortable to work with. Many United States florists mainly use the floral knife. This knife is suitable for working with the speed necessary to make a large number of floral arrangements in a limited amount of time, as required in the flower business. When using a new tool, it's important to practice using it until you are comfortable with it.

Some flower-arranging tools. From left to right: kenzan, transparent tape, bowl, green floral wire, 16-gauge wire, ikebana scissors

Kenzan

The kenzan is used with the moribana style of arrangement and is typically placed in a shallow container to help support the flowers in the container. It's important to choose the right size kenzan for the quantity of materials used in the arrangement: If the kenzan is too small for the materials, it won't hold them securely. If the kenzan is too big, it's hard to cover the kenzan (it's strictly a functional tool and needs covering in the finished arrangement). Choose the size and shape appropriate to the size and shape of your container. I mainly use the round one because it works well with most containers, although the kenzan may also be rectangular or square. Kenzans and ikebana scissors can be found in the United States; look for these tools at stores that specialize in Japanese goods. You may also find them online. (See "Resources" on page 110.)

16-Gauge Wire

Wire can be used as support for the nageire style of arrangement. The wire is formed into a ball and placed into a container to hold plant materials. I usually make a rough ball-shaped wire by loosely coiling a thin (16-gauge) wire around my hand a few times. This wire is available at most hardware stores. If a more complex shape is necessary to hold the materials, I'll make a few smaller wire balls and place them together in the container. Doing this allows thinner stems to be held in the wire more firmly.

Green Florist's Wire

When I make ikebana I usually use green florist's wire, typically found in most arts and crafts supply stores. This type of wire is very useful for ikebana techniques such as attaching a splint to thin flower stems or binding together several stems (see the technique section for a detailed explanation). I usually will only coil the wire a few times around each stem. If you use too much wire or coil it too tight, the stems may be broken. If it is difficult to find the green florist's wire, regular transparent tape can be used as a substitute to bind a group of thin stems.

Other Materials

Beyond these basic tools of ikebana and flower arranging, you may find these next items handy for adding finishing touches to your arrangements or for use in special containers.

Small Stones

I sometimes use gravel or small stones to hide the kenzan in a container. They look nice with fresh flowers because they are natural materials. I try not to use too fine of a gravel to hide the kenzan, because small stones can easily get stuck between the needles on the kenzan and take extra time to clean up.

Marbles

In Western-style arrangements, marbles are often used in glass containers to support plant materials or for decoration. I sometimes use marbles to make ikebana in glass containers. When choosing marbles for an arrangement, be aware of how their color will affect your over-all design. Personally, I prefer matching clear glass marbles with most containers and materials.

Floral Water Tubes

The water tube is one of the tools often used to keep flowers fresh, particularly in Western-style floral arrangements. The water tubes can provide water to fresh flowers when other means for delivering water, such as floral foam, aren't practical. Use only one flower per tube, and check every few days to make sure that water remains in the tube after you finish the arrangement. An arrangement showing the use of floral water tubes is described in the step-by-step section.

Floral Foam

Floral foam is used mainly in Western-style floral arrangements. However, I often use this material for arrangements that need to be portable, such as gift baskets. You can usually buy this foam at a flower shop.

To use floral foam, first place the foam in a bucket of fresh water and wait until it's soaking wet. Next, cut the foam to fit the shape of the container you are using. (When I use a basket, I'll place a plastic liner inside to keep water from leaking out.) Finally, insert the stems of the flowers into the foam, taking care to ensure that the foam is completely covered by foliage or flowers. Your materials can more easily be inserted into the foam if the stems are cut diagonally. Never use foam more than once, and check it periodically to make sure that it stays wet.

These are additional items I often use to create ikebana. Clockwise from top: floral foam, small stones, marbles, and floral tubes.

Ikebana Techniques

Following are some fundamental ikebana techniques that you must know when creating ikebana arrangements. These techniques have three functions: (1) to keep the materials fresh, (2)
to allow the materials to be cut easily, and (3) to support the materials in the container. There
are numerous types of ikebana arrangements, ranging from the classic style to the contemporary. Regardless of the type of arrangement, however, you must master the fundamental techniques in order to construct the basic form.

Preparing Plant Materials

Before starting your arrangement, it's important to prepare the materials you're planning to
use. Taking proper care to prepare your plant materials will help keep the materials fresh and
also greatly enhance the overall look of your finished arrangements. The following preparatory
techniques involve some of the most basic skills for making ikebana.

Mizukiri, a water-absorption technique

Water Absorption (Mizukiri)

Mizukiri means "to cut the stem underwater." This is the standard technique used to keep flowers fresher longer, and it works for many types of flowers. Cutting the stems underwater causes
the stem to absorb water instead of air.

Cleaning Leaves

For the preparation of foliage, I wipe the surface of the leaves with a wet paper towel prior to making the arrangement. Clean leaves add a freshness to the arrangement.

Cleaning leaves

Preparing Branches

A clean line is important for the form of an arrangement. When using branches as the form for your arrangement, consider the shape of the branches carefully. Select a sturdy branch as the main line rather than one of the thin branches.

To make the line cleaner, you should trim any broken or excess twigs from your branch. If there are other branches splitting off from the main branch, keep the strongest or best-shaped branch to use as the main line, and trim off the other ones. Keep the excess branches to use as additional lines if needed.

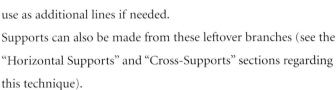

Trimming a branch

Removing excess leaves

Supports can also be made from these leftover branches (see the "Horizontal Supports" and "Cross-Supports" sections regarding this technique).

You should also remove excess leaves from the stems before making an arrangement, especially leaves below the water line. This keeps the arrangement clean looking and helps maintain the water content in fresh flowers. Removing the leaves below the water line also helps protect against bacterial growth. (Note: You should also carefully remove the old petals from flowers.)

Bending a branch

The technique of bending branches is also often used in ikebana to create a shaped line in the arrangement. To bend a branch, use both hands to gently curve the branch, starting in the center and moving outward toward the ends.

Cutting

It's important to master the correct cutting techniques. These techniques will help you to cut your materials without difficulty and shape them so they attach securely to a device, such as a kenzan or a container. Different cutting techniques are used for different plant materials and for different types of containers.

Cutting a Branch

Cut a branch diagonally because this requires less force. The diagonal cut is also more stable when attached to a kenzan for a moribana-style arrangement (using a shallow container with the kenzan). It can also be fixed more securely on the inside wall of a tall vase for the nageire-style arrangement (using a tall vase without the kenzan).

Cut branches diagonally

Cutting a Flower

For the moribana style, I cut the stems of flowers straight (flat). The straight-cut end of the stems is more easily stabilized on the kenzan. For the nageire style, I usually cut the stems of flowers diagonally. The diagonally cut stem can be fixed more securely against the inside wall of a vase.

When using a kenzan as the mechanics for your arrangement, it's important to use the proper technique for securing plant materials to the kenzan. Here are some basic, yet important, techniques on how to correctly place branches and flowers on the kenzan.

Above: Cut flower stems diagonally when using a vase.

Left: Cut flower stems straight across when using a kenzan.

Placing a Branch on a Kenzan

To place a branch on a kenzan, hold the diagonally cut branch with both hands and force it straight down onto the kenzan. Be careful not to hit your hand on the kenzan spikes! After the branch is securely affixed to the kenzan, tilt the branch to the angle that you prefer.

Hold the branch with both hands and push it straight onto the kenzan.

Once the branch is secure, bend it to the angle you desire.

Placing a Flower on a Kenzan

Trim the flower to the desired length using a straight cut. Remove any excess leaves from the stem. Look at the shape of the flower closely to find the side of the flower that you feel is the most beautiful. Flowers, much like individuals, each have a different face and can appear more attractive if viewed from a certain direction, such as from the front or in profile. Affix the flower to the kenzan facing the direction you feel best suits the flower and the arrangement.

If the stem of a flower or foliage is too thin to be fixed onto the kenzan, there are some techniques you can use to work around this problem.

Place the flower on the kenzan at the angle you desire.

Caps

If your flower's stem is too thin, you can make a "cap" from a larger flower stem of sufficient strength and thickness. Insert the thin stem into the cap, and then place it on the kenzan. This will help anchor it onto the kenzan.

Insert a cap onto a thin-stemmed flower. The cap helps secure the flower on the kenzan.

Splint

To bulk up a thin stem, you can also create a splint. Cut an approximately 2-inch piece of stem of sufficient sturdiness to form a splint. (The length of the splint should vary depending on the length of the thin stem.) Cut the splint in two down the middle. Attach the flat side of the splint to the bottom of the thin stem and tie the two together with florist's wire. Coil the wire a few times around the top and bottom of the splint. Trim the base of the

Add a splint to a thin-stemmed flower.

The splint helps secure the flower on the kenzan.

stem so that it is even with the splint, and attach them both to the kenzan.

If you can't find a thick stem to use for the splint, simply do not cut the splint in half. Just attach the splint to the lower part of the thin flower stem and tie the two together with florist's wire.

You can also use a full stem as a splint. Secure the flower with the splint to the kenzan.

Binding a Group of Thin-Stemmed Flowers

I keep the short-, thin-, or broken-stemmed flowers when I make an arrangement, because they can be used to cover the kenzan or add volume to an arrangement. A group of such flowers can be tied together with green florist's wire or regular transparent tape. When you use wire, you need to be careful not to coil it around the stems too hard. A few times is enough. Cut the base of the stems evenly (flat), which makes them easier to attach to the kenzan.

Bind a group of thin-stemmed flowers together with wire. Secure the group onto the kenzan.

Supporting Techniques

When creating the nageire style of ikebana, we hold the materials in the vase by means of floral mechanics (basic support techniques) other than using a kenzan. Following are some examples of basic ikebana techniques used in the nageire style.

Horizontal Supports

Horizontal supports may be used to help shore up the plant materials in a vase. Make a support by cutting a branch or firm stem (about the diameter of a pencil, if possible) approximately the same length as the diameter at the mouth of the vase. You may want to cut a slightly longer support if this fits better in the container. Place the support horizontally within the mouth of the vase. This technique is suitable for an opaque vase, but should not be used with a thin glass or transparent vase.

A horizontal support holding a split branch

A horizontal support

A horizontal support can also be used to hold a split branch when using branches in the arrangement. Wire may additionally be used for further reinforcement, if necessary.

Cross-Supports

If one horizontal support is insufficient to hold the materials in the container, another support may be added crosswise for extra support. Create two supports by cutting a branch or strong stem into two equal parts approximately the same length as the diameter of the vase. Place the two supports perpendicular to one another to form a cross-support in the mouth of the vase. Tie the center using florist's wire if you think it's necessary. (Note: Do not attempt this technique if using a delicate glass vase since it may become damaged. It is more suitable for an opaque vase.)

A cross-support

This is the basic mechanic involved in using wire. Make a loose ball shape using 16-gauge wire and place it inside a container of relatively large width. The shaped wire will support both flowers and branches placed in the container. The wire ball should be hidden inside of the container—I usually keep it under the water level.

The length of the wire can vary depending on the size of the container, and you can wind it tighter or squeeze it together for added density if necessary to support a larger quantity of materials. To support a large number of thin stems, for example, I would make the ball denser, while I'd make the ball less dense to support just a few stems.

A wire support

Fixing a Stem without a Support

Many times stems can be fixed in place without using a support by cutting the stems diagonally. Place each flower inside of the container with the cut end touching the container's inside surface. Add additional stems crosswise to one another because this will help secure the materials firmly inside the container.

Using a diagonal cut to support a stem

Helpful Hints

Here are some hints that generally apply to making any floral arrangement. You should find them helpful when creating your own ikebana.

Keeping Your Flowers Fresh

Your flowers will stay fresh longer if you trim their stems underwater right after you bring them home. (See the water absorption technique.) If you don't make an arrangement right away, be sure to keep your flowers in a bucket of fresh water and then cut their stems underwater again before you use them.

Large Container

If I'm using a large or heavy container, I'll place a smaller container inside of it in which I actually make the arrangement. The smaller container better supports the materials and makes it easier to change the water.

Location of Flower Arrangement

Avoid direct sunlight or heat when you display flowers. During the summertime, I'll also put a couple of ice cubes into the container and spray water on the flowers occasionally to help keep them fresh, especially if I'm delivering the flowers somewhere.

Add a small container to a larger one to make it easier to change the water.

Use of Irregular Materials

Sometimes flower stems can break while you are arranging them, or you have leftover flowers with other imperfections. These flowers may still be helpful to cover the mechanics used or to add volume to the arrangement, or they can stand separately in a small container.

Viewer Perspective

When the intended site for your ikebana arrangement is lower than eye level, say for instance on a coffee table, you may want to use a basin or shallow container. Because the viewer will look down to see the arrangement, this allows you to use the inside of the basin as part of the design.

This type of arrangement is suitable for a lower type of table because it is designed for display below eye level. Galax leaves and stones at the bottom of the container become part of the design. The green galax floating inside the container, set against the black stones viewed between the galax and the one orange carnation, make a harmonious color combination with the other materials used.

This arrangement could be used for the dining table, because it is designed to be viewed from a higher perspective and won't take up too much space on the table. Do not use too tall of an arrangement for your dining room table, however, because it will interfere with people's conversation. Similarly, if the flowers are too fragrant this will detract from people's enjoyment of the food.

Ikebana is ordinarily designed for a specific site and not for delivery from one place to another. However, an ikebana-style arrangement makes an attractive gift when created in a portable basket.

Here's an example of a portable basket arrangement. It's small and light for easy delivery. Floral foam is used to support the flowers inside of the basket.

I kebana is a three-dimensional form that uses natural materials arranged to create a sense of space and depth. Much as a sculptor creates a three-dimensional form using clay, wood, or metal, we use the given shape of our natural materials to create the form of our ikebana. The main difference between ikebana and other kinds of art, such as sculpture, is that the materials we use already have a definite shape and color. Another defining characteristic is that the materials themselves have life, but will only last temporarily.

Your ikebana form will be created by using three main elements: lines, volume (consisting of depth and mass), and an accent or focal point. Beyond these elements, there are also specific design principles that you must consider; these include shape, balance, and positive and negative space.

Original arrangement

This photograph shows the line element in this arrangement.

Line

The ikebana form is ordinarily kept rather minimal, in order to best show the natural beauty of the plant materials. To accomplish this, the emphasis in the form is placed on lines rather than on an abundance of materials. The lines used in your arrangement will create the movement in your form.

Just as there are innumerable different lines we can use when drawing on blank paper, many different lines may potentially be used in creating ikebana.

■ The use of straight horizontal and vertical lines creates a rather static effect. This is an example of a strong horizontal line. It lends a quality of stillness to the arrangement. **(Opposite, top)**

■ You can also add more complicated lines and effects by mixing different lines in one ikebana form. This arrangement combines multiple types of lines. Two kinds of lines (straight lines of horsetail and natural lines of curly willow) are used in one arrangement. **(Opposite, bottom)**

The use of geometric lines, including radiating or triangular lines, gives balanced weight to the form. This arrangement is an example of using lines radiating from a center point. The geometric lines add an equal, balanced weight to the form.

This arrangement shows a sculptural form made of bent lines using natural materials. More lines were added at multiple angles to generate depth and complication in the form. Much as we create perspective in painting, I used taller and thicker lines in the front area and smaller lines in the back area to add depth to the form of this arrangement.

The use of curved, circular, and diagonal lines adds dynamic movement to the form. This arrangement is an example of the use of curved lines. The variation between the large and small circular lines creates the movement. **(Opposite)**

Aspidistra, curly willow, and tepe are materials that I typically use for my line construction.

I generally use branches, foliage, or some flower stems for the line construction. The branch is the most commonly used material for creating lines in traditional ikebana. When choosing foliage for the line construction, use a piece with enough length to create the line. When choosing flower stems for the line, choose stems that have some stability or thickness.

When you make a freestyle arrangement, there are no rules about the number of lines or what angles you may use. You can make an arrangement using only one line or any number of lines. The more lines you use, obviously, the more complicated your line construction will become.

No matter how many lines you use for the line construction, however, always choose your main line first, because the height of the main line will determine the overall size of the arrangement. The taller your main line is, the taller the rest of your materials should be in proportion. Establish the height of the main line after taking into consideration the desired size of your arrangement in proportion to your container and the site. Your main line can be a branch, foliage, or a thick, stable flower stem.

Volume (Mass and Depth)

Volume gives solid depth to the ikebana form. Volume also adds visual weight. I usually use flowers that already have heavy volume or mass. Certain flowers, for instance, grow together, with many small flowers in one cluster. Some kinds of foliage can also provide volume when used with bending, twisting, or folding

This photograph illustrates the volume element.

techniques. In this case, remember to choose foliage that has sufficient width and flexibility, such as aspidistra or hala.

Volume can be used as the form's main element or as a secondary element. When using the volume as the form's main element, always consider the relationship between the container and the volume. If too much volume is used for a small container, the arrangement becomes too heavy looking. If too little volume is used in a large container, the arrangement will lack the qualities of depth and mass.

When I add volume along the line construction, the line element becomes the main element and the volume a secondary element. Be sure not to inadvertently cover the line construction when adding volume in this way as a secondary element.

Tree fern, pompon cushion, and aspidistra are some examples of volume materials that I often use.

This photograph highlights the accent element.

Accent

The accent is the final added touch that captures the viewer's attention and becomes the focal point of your arrangement. It should be created by using some feature that you want to emphasize or highlight. The accent is usually the color or shape of the flowers (one flower or more than one flower). A unique texture can also serve as the accent. The accent is like the spice used in a recipe. With this final element the arrangement will come to life. However, too much accent material relative to the line and volume elements creates more of a decoration than an accent.

I usually use flowers rather than foliage for my accent materials. Any flowers can become the accent or focal point, but I usually choose the flower(s) with a distinctive color or strong contrast against the other materials for the accent.

How the accent is added to the arrangement depends on your personal taste, much like selecting an accessory as the final touch for an outfit. I usually prefer using a simple accent. When I use only a few flowers for the accent, I often choose complementary colors to create a color contrast.

Other Elements of Design

Shape, balance, and the use of space are important elements in any kind of design work. They must also be considered in making ikebana, in addition to the line, volume, and accent elements.

A natural-looking arrangement that utilizes the characteristic shapes of the materials.

Shape

Each branch, piece of foliage, and flower stem has its own characteristic shape. In both ikebana and Western floral arrangements, we can either use the natural shapes that nature provides us or manipulate the natural materials into our desired shape. There are three primary shapes used for ikebana.

The Natural Shape

We can emphasize the natural beauty in an arrangement by using our materials just as they are. A beautiful, organic-looking arrangement can be made using the natural shapes in the vase.

The Manipulated Shape (Curved, Bent, Twisted, or Folded)

Natural materials such as branches or leaves can be manipulated into different shapes if the materials we choose have flexibility. For example, we can create a curved line or create volume by twisting the leaves if they are soft and flexible, or can fold the leaves and stems to create a geometric shape.

Artificial Shapes

I sometimes use artificial materials such as paper, fabricated wood products such as wooden sticks, or plastic to help shape my ikebana form. The combination of artificial and natural shapes leads to unique results.

I usually use artificial shapes as an alternative line or volume element. There are many possible materials that will work. Rolled-up paper, for example, can serve as the volume element, while thin wooden sticks can be the line element. Overuse of artificial shapes, however, will distract from the beauty of your flowers and other natural materials.

There are no particular rules for determining the actual shape of your arrangement. Just let your inspiration and own sense of aesthetics guide you. For instance, you may decide that the use of artificial shapes fits nicely with a modern interior.

This is an example of a manipulated shape. Aspidistra leaves are soft enough to be curved and are used to add volume in this arrangement.

This is an example of the use of asymmetrical balance. The right and left sides of the arrangement are not equal; the left side has more visual weight than the right side.

Balance

The unique character of the ikebana form is that it is based upon asymmetrical (uneven, irregular) balance rather than symmetrical (even, proportioned) balance. For example, the heights of branches will be different or more materials will be used on one side than on the other side, thus giving more visual weight to one side than the other. This asymmetrical form creates the rhythm (movement) in the arrangement. For instance, movement is created when the materials vary from short to tall or from a large mass to a thin line. The use of asymmetrical balance can also be found in the conventional Japanese garden consisting of rocks, sand, and trees.

This is an example of the use of symmetrical balance. The right and left sides of the arrangement have almost the same visual weight and balance.

This stick made of paperboard (an artificial material) is combined with other, natural materials in this arrangement. The stick creates a strong horizontal line.

The height, thickness, and placement of the materials will determine the degree of symmetrical or asymmetrical balance in your arrangement. Varying the height of the line or accent elements, or varying the placement of the volume or accent elements between different sides of the arrangement will create asymmetrical balance, while keeping the elements distributed evenly creates symmetrical balance.

One of the important aesthetics of ikebana is the overall balance between the positive space, or the space physically occupied by the ikebana, and the negative space. The negative space, or the emptiness forming the background of the ikebana, is also part of the design. This use of positive and negative space can often be seen in the traditional Japanese art forms, such as brushed ink painting. In traditional Japanese painting, the painter creates a tension between the ink or paint brushed onto the paper and the surrounding emptiness.

Positive space and negative space are interrelated; more positive space equals less negative space, and vice versa. I think that what makes ikebana design interesting is how we contrast these types of space.

The use of lines is an important factor in creating both positive and negative space in your design. If the arrangement consists only of thick volume, the positive and negative space will exist separately. If lines are used to create the form, however, the empty or negative space between the lines becomes part of the design. Even one lengthy, strong curved line set against otherwise empty space, for example, creates a compelling tension between the positive and negative space.

The relationship between the positive and negative space is also created by the transition from the volume (mass) to the lines. An essential aspect of ikebana design is the asymmetrical transition from mass to line.

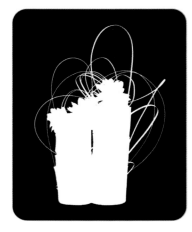

Be aware of the positive and negative space in your ikebana. The illustration at the left shows the positive space occupied by the ikebana; the illustration at the right shows the negative space surrounding the ikebana.

Considering Plant Materials

The plant materials you use will obviously affect the overall design of your arrangement. I usually will use only two or three different kinds of materials, and I prefer to use a minimal quantity of materials in order to emphasize the quality and character of each flower. I'll examine the shape, color, texture, and density of each piece carefully. Each characteristic of our materials provides us with different options and can inspire ideas about the ikebana form.

Shape

Each variety of flower, foliage, or branch has its own characteristic shape, of course. The shapes of natural materials are much more intricate and interesting than those we could create ourselves. Some are round (allium); others are pointed (snapdragon), while many have their own uniquely distinctive shape (heliconia, anthurium).

Color

The variations of color found in nature are practically beyond the imagination. Some flowers are only one color, while others are composed of several colors. You will find varying hues even among the same types of flowers in the same color group. Because ordinarily only a few different kinds of materials are used in a given ikebana arrangement, it is important to select the color of each piece carefully.

Texture

Texture is a key element of our materials, and there are countless different textures to choose from. Some flowers or foliage have a smooth texture like the lily, a shiny texture like anthurium, or a velvet texture like certain varieties of roses.

Density

Natural materials vary greatly in terms of their density, and this affects how they can be used. Hard materials are suitable for making geometric shapes or forms consisting of straight lines. Soft and pliable or thin materials may be fashioned into bent or curved shapes.

The Process of Making Ikebana

Now that you have a sense of the design elements involved in creating ikebana, the following step-by-step descriptions will illustrate the process of making ikebana using the three basic design elements of line, volume, and accent. I use the same materials to show how two different styles of arrangement, moribana and nageire, can be created using the basic design elements.

Choose your Site, Container, and Materials

The appearance of your ikebana arrangement is a function of your materials, site, and container, as well as your own aesthetic. Your main concept will generally come from your choices of these features, and these selections will affect the other elements of your design. You may have an initial idea for your ikebana, for instance, and then select the site, container, and materials based on this idea. Here are some examples of how you might approach a design.

- The choice of materials may determine your main idea. You may find materials that you like based on the season or occasion and then select a container and site suitable for these materials.

- The choice of the site where you would like to display your arrangement may provide your main idea. If you already know the site for the display, you can choose the materials and container to match this site.

- The choice of the container can also provide your main idea. You may have a favorite container, or you may have made your own container and will then design the arrangement around this container.

Even if I don't have a concrete idea, I'll just select a container that matches my materials and will start making the ikebana form. My interaction with the materials during the process of making the arrangement guides how I proceed. Closely observing the shape of the materials often provides my creative inspiration. Don't think too hard about your idea; just try and visualize the shape that best fits your materials.

Moribana Style

As mentioned earlier, the moribana style is one of the most basic and common ikebana styles found in use today. We use a shallow container along with a kenzan to hold the materials inside. Since the kenzan is used for this style, we must know the basic techniques for how to cut the materials and attach them firmly to the kenzan. (These techniques are shown in the "Ikebana Techniques" section in chapter 1). You can use more than one container, and more than one kenzan per container, depending upon the design of your arrangement.

Three Elements of Ikebana Composition—Line, Volume, and Accent

STEP 1

STEP 2

STEP 3

Here is an example of line construction using horsetail as the material. The creation of the lines determines the overall size of the arrangement. The sturdiest and longest stem was chosen as the main line and placed on the kenzan first. Other lines were added along the main line. The rectangular form was created using multiple lines. The form was given depth by adding lines at multiple angles.

Here is an example of how volume was added to the lines. In this arrangement, the solidago (yellow flowers) were added on only the left side. (It would be too thick and heavy looking if I added volume to both sides.) The added volume also covered the kenzan.

Here is an example of how yellow roses are arranged to create the accent. They are placed along the lines and within the volume. The spiral pattern of the accent also adds movement to the form.

STEP 1: CONSTRUCT THE LINE

Decide the size of the arrangement by cutting the material for the main line and starting the framework of the form. When I use more than one line in my arrangement, I'll usually choose the sturdiest line as the main line to begin the construction and add additional lines to create the framework.

STEP 2: ADD VOLUME

Add mass or depth to provide volume to your line construction. When adding volume to the line, take into account the proportion (quantity and height) of the materials relative to the line. Try and find a balance so that the volume is neither too bulky nor too light compared to the line.

STEP 3: CREATE THE ACCENT

Add the accent to create the focal point of the arrangement by adding color, shape, or texture. When the accent is added, the arrangement will be complete.

Two Elements of Ikebana Composition—Line and Accent

STEP 1	STEP 2

Here is an example of line construction. The largest triangle is formed as the main line to define the size of the arrangement, and other lines are added along the main line. Multiple triangles create the overall geometric form.

All the leaves were removed from the roses to show the clear lines in this arrangement. The different length roses were added as the accent and give rhythm to the form.

STEP 1: CONSTRUCT THE LINE

First construct the form of the ikebana using the line.

STEP 2: ADD THE ACCENT

Next, add your accent to complete the arrangement.

Two Elements of Ikebana Composition—Volume and Accent

STEP 1

STEP 2

Here is an example how volume is created as the first step. It's important to think about the quantity of the volume relative to the size of the container.

Next, the accent is added to the volume. I arranged some roses within the volume and added one tall rose. This creates a visual harmony because the bottom has more visual weight than the top.

STEP 1: CONSTRUCT THE VOLUME

First construct the volume element to produce depth in the arrangement.

STEP 2: ADD THE ACCENT

Add the accent to complete the arrangement.

One Element of Ikebana Composition—Accent Only

STEP 1

This is a simple way to make an arrangement using only one element (the accent). Short-stemmed roses are arranged in a shallow container. The short roses and the gravel help cover the kenzan. This single-element type of arrangement can be made from a small quantity of materials, such as the flowers left over from another arrangement.

STEP 1: ADD THE ACCENT

You can create ikebana using only one element. This kind of arrangement is suitable for a limited space or a small container.

Summary

There are no rules about how to combine the elements or how many materials you can use. Once you become comfortable making three-dimensional forms using the line, volume, and accent elements, you can enjoy creating any forms that you like by combining different materials and elements.

Some materials can also serve as "dual elements," particularly if grouped together. A group of lines, for instance, may act primarily as a line element but additionally give depth to the form as a volume element. Similarly, a distinctive group of flowers can act as both the accent and volume elements.

Nageire Style

As mentioned previously, nageire is another common style of ikebana practiced today. For this style, we use an upright vase and support techniques other than the kenzan. (These are introduced in the support section of chapter 1.) It is important for you to understand how to support the materials in the container in order to create your desired form.

Three Elements of Ikebana Composition—Fan Form

STEP 1: CONSTRUCT THE LINE

Myrtle branches are arranged symmetrically in the shape of a fan. This arrangement is tall and wide, making it suitable for a spacious site. The extra length of the lines keeps the form proportionate to the tall container.

STEP 2: CONSTRUCT THE VOLUME

Baby's breath is used for volume at the center of the lines. In this arrangement the lines are placed rather flat, like the shape of a fan, so I add the baby's breath in the shape of a ball to create depth.

STEP 3: ADD THE ACCENT

The violet flowers (Aster Matsumoto) were added as the accent. This is a small flower, but it has strong complementary colors (violet/yellow) in each flower. The colors of these flowers become the accent in this arrangement.

Two Elements of Ikebana Composition–Ball Form

STEP 1: CONSTRUCT THE VOLUME

Baby's breath creates the ball-shaped volume. I made the volume thick to match the tall vase.

STEP 2: ADD THE ACCENT

Aster Matsumoto are placed evenly amid the volume as the accent. In this example, the symmetrical form is completed with two elements.

Two Elements of Ikebana Composition–Asymmetrical Form

STEP 1: CONSTRUCT THE LINE

Myrtle branches are arranged in asymmetrical lines pointed in one direction.

STEP 2: ADD THE ACCENT

Aster Matsumoto is arranged as the accent. The asters are placed as a group to maintain visual balance against the asymmetrical lines. A few flowers are arranged along these lines to create the relationship between the lines and the accent. The large group of asters also gives depth to the form.

STEP ONE: ADD THE ACCENT
Here is an arrangement consisting only of the accent element and using two different kinds of flowers. This arrangement is very simple, and it is about the color. The Aster Matsumoto and the green chrysanthemum are placed in two roughly equal halves in a ball form.

Summary

I hope that these examples of the moribana and nageire styles have helped you to understand how each style was created using the basic design elements of line, volume, and accent. Please try to create your own ikebana once you're confident that you grasp the basic elements and techniques.

Sometimes I'll sketch out my rough ideas before making ikebana. Other times I'll listen to music while making an arrangement to help my sense of rhythm. Similarly, you should work in whatever manner you feel most comfortable with. Again, these are freestyle ikebana arrangements, and your work will be entirely your own, so don't worry too much about following a rigid plan. Enjoy yourself!

"Ideas" and "inspiration" sound like similar concepts, but though they are connected to one another, I believe that they can also be described separately. Ideas are rather logical, whereas inspiration is much more intuitive.

An idea is something we can put on paper to convey our concept to other people. For instance, we can draw an image of the finished ikebana form we intend to make. We can also plan the size of the arrangement and select the site, the container, and the materials before making our ikebana. This deliberate thought and planning is all based on ideas.

What is inspiration? Inspiration is not something we can plan or prepare. It usually comes to us spontaneously by way of some influence and is improvisational. The freestyle method of ikebana arrangement draws on both ideas and inspiration in the same way as other art forms.

I believe that each ikebana designer has his or her own way of thinking about ideas and finding inspiration. For instance, each designer has his or her own approach to developing the form when making a freestyle arrangement. Some of them carefully plan concrete ideas for the selection of the site, containers, materials, and the form before they start making an arrangement, and then simply follow through on their original ideas to complete the form. Others might start making ikebana without any plan and subsequently develop their ideas and inspiration during the process of making the arrangement.

The extent to which you plan your work can often depend upon the arrangement itself. If your general idea involves a very large or complicated form, it may require a careful plan. There is no order for how we work with our ideas and inspiration. I think it is most important to work the way that we feel is most natural. Let us listen to our creative intuition and follow it. How often in our daily lives do we get the opportunity to just follow our creativity where it leads us?

To me, one of the most interesting things about making a freestyle ikebana arrangement is the experience "happening" during the process of making the form. It is almost like improvisational artwork. Once I have any kind of an idea—even just a rough idea—of my design, I'll start working with the materials. I usually get my inspiration during the process of making ikebana, and this guides me to complete the form.

My inspiration comes from my interaction with the natural materials—observing their shape, color, and features as well as the expression of each flower. My inspiration also comes from feeling the texture and pliability of the materials. The features of the branches, foliage, and flowers give me answers about how I should transform these natural materials into my ikebana form. Even if I cut the stems too short, break a stem, or bend a branch too much, there's always an answer for how to best put together the form of the arrangement. These answers given from the natural materials are what I call my inspiration.

Sometimes I can pursue my intended form based on my original idea. Other times, my finished piece is completely different from my original idea. The fresh, organic materials offer plentiful options and provide "improvisational inspiration" to me. The freestyle method allows me to change the form during the process of making the arrangement if my original idea doesn't work. Unlike working with metal and wood, which requires that I plan the exact size and shape of the materials before creating my form, working with organic materials to make ikebana requires no such detailed planning.

I also think it is important to be in a creative environment and looking outward for inspiration to help along your creative process. I try to go to museums, various exhibitions, or concert and dance recitals. Looking at sculpture and paintings helps me to learn about form and color. The music and dance helps me develop a better sense of rhythm and movement. I believe that it is the accumulation of all these creative experiences that becomes the source for my inspiration and my ideas later on. Overall, freestyle ikebana is derived from a combination of color, form, and rhythm and our own individual creativity.

Keiko's Ikebana Gallery

The following ten arrangements introduce some of my current ikebana works. I include a brief description of the design and construction process involved in making these arrangements, including: my initial ideas, the design elements, my thoughts on ikebana generally, and the experimental element in each design. Hopefully, these arrangements will serve as some inspiration for creating your own unique ikebana designs.

Right: In this example, I started making the arrangement with the rough idea of using shredded leaves and was then inspired to shape the shredded foliage like entwined strings into a nestlike form.

Materials:

Steel grass

Baby's breath

Allium

Container: Fabricated metal containers

When I make a sculptural piece, I often work with metal as the medium. My idea is to mix industrial materials, such as metal, with the natural materials for my ikebana arrangement. I fabricated these metal containers as an experiment to test this idea. The thin steel grass draws an overlapping curved line between the two containers. Baby's breath is used to add the volume, and these small delicate flowers help make the violet color of the alliums stand out more distinctly. The alliums are used as an accent element to create the focal point in the form. The combination of two extremely different materials—the hard, machine-made containers and the soft, organic materials—creates the unique-looking result.

Gallery Arrangement 2

Materials:

Allium

Violet paper

Paperboard sticks

Container: Fabricated wire mesh

This idea came from seeing how far I can go to minimize the materials used in making an arrangement. Simplicity (or minimalism) is something that I am always seeking in my artwork as well as my ikebana works. This arrangement is created through a combination of the geometric forms: the round allium, the cylindrical form made out of wire (the violet paper is used inside one of the cylinders), and the straight lines made out of paperboard sticks.

Natural materials already have beautiful intrinsic shapes and colors. The balance between how much I should manipulate a material's shape and how much I should use its own natural shape is one of the most difficult decisions for me when I make ikebana. Too much manipulation will ruin the beauty of the natural materials, just as too much added decoration will ruin the beauty of anything.

Materials:

Sunflower

Yellow rose

Craspedia

Solidago

Aspidistra

Container: Three square glass containers
containing clear marbles

The subject of this arrangement is the use of mono-chromatic color. I don't usually mix sunflowers and roses together because both of them have a distinctive shape. However, in this arrangement, I experimented with mixing these flowers with others that have a yellow hue. Green leaves (aspidistra) are used for contrast. When using materials of varying shapes in one arrange-ment, I try to minimize the use of color so that they don't look too crowded.

Hala leaves are used as the line element in this arrangement. Some hala leaves are used with their natural lines intact, while others have been folded. Baby's breath is added for the volume element. The accent element is formed by the complementary color scheme of red and green anthuriums.

Materials:

Hala leaves

Anthurium

Baby's breath

Container: Two tall green containers

There are many ways of arranging materials in two containers. My style is usually to add more materials to one container than the other, which is the approach I took in this instance in order to create the asymmetrical balance seen here. One of the most noticeable characteristics of ikebana is that, more often than not, its form manifests asymmetrical balance rather than symmetrical balance.

Materials:

Dahlia

Aspidistra

Steel grass

**Container: Aspidistra leaves wrapped
around two cylindrical containers**

There are practically an unlimited number of ways that we can use foliage. Foliage is typically a flexible material easily manipulated from an ordinary flat shape into other forms. It is my favorite material, and one I use often in my arrangements. This arrangement includes aspidistra leaves that wrap around and cover the container. Looped lines of steel grass add the depth and movement. Three dahlias are used as a strong color accent against the green of the foliage.

The longer I have worked with lines to produce ikebana, the more I have learned to notice if a line has life to it or not. It doesn't matter if the line is curved, straight, or just a natural line (straight lines generally look static, while curved lines project more movement). What matters is whether or not the line has energy. A lively line that has energy is what makes the arrangement itself come alive.

The main idea comes from a basket and two sake bottles that I brought from Japan. I wanted to make a form linking the three containers in one arrangement, and the dynamic arched lines of steel grass and curved stems of the calla lilies are used to that effect here. Queen Anne's lace is added to the basket container for volume. The calla lilies also serve as a color accent.

Materials:

Calla lily

Steel grass

Queen Anne's lace

Container: Basket and sake bottles

When I use curved lines, I like to visualize large dynamic lines for my design because this helps stir my imagination. On the other hand, I sometimes have trouble envisioning new ideas if I must create too small of an arrangement to fit in a tighter space. Having a larger space to work with definitely loosens up my creativity. I also tend to believe in the importance of letting air into your ikebana. Instead of making a tight and rigid arrangement, I try to draw sweeping lines in the air.

The natural lines of grass double as radiated lines expanding outward from the center of this arrangement. Tree fern is used to give the form volume. The strong color and features of the dendrobiums are used as an accent element against the simple silver vase, and a large group of dendrobiums lend volume as well. Since the form of this arrangement is basically symmetrical, I use the scattered leaves and flowers to relax the composition and make it less formal. The dendrobiums and galax leaves resting on the table are also reflected on the silver colored vase, adding an interesting pattern to the design.

Materials:

Dendrobium

Steel grass

Tree fern

Galax leaves

Container: Large glass vase

Colorful gerbera and hypericum are placed inside of small, cupped shapes made from aspidistra leaves. My idea came from looking at the vibrant colors of the gerbera. The variations of pink and orange gerbera reminded me of a painter's palette. It was like selecting my favorite color from the paint palette, and sometimes it can be difficult to choose only one. I wanted to use all of them but I tried to avoid mixing all of these beautiful colors. Instead of making the arrangement in a container, I placed them on the table next to each other. This way, each differently colored gerbera is presented clearly.

Materials:

Gerbera

Aspidistra

Horsetail

Hypericum

Materials:

Carnation

Curly willow

Purple majesty (ornamental millet)

Container: Tall brown ceramic container

Two types of the lines are used in this arrangement. One type of line is the natural curved line of the curly willow, and the other type is the straight line of the purple majesty (sometimes called ornamental millet). A large group of carnations add the thick ball-shaped volume. Orange carnations also form the color accent element against the brown container.

My idea came from the color of the purple majesty. When I found this material, I knew immediately that I wanted to use the brown vase of the same color. Then I chose the orange carnations to match the vase. This very simple form consists of a combination of geometric forms: the cone shape of the brown container, the ball-shaped carnations, and the straight lines of purple majesty. The symmetrical form is crafted from these different geometric elements. To finish the arrangement, I added the natural curved lines of curly willow to help break the rigidity of the symmetrical form.

The complicated lines are what distinguish this arrangement. Triangles made from horsetail are arranged in a zigzag pattern between three small containers. This pattern generates an alternating rhythm that draws the viewer's attention both inside and outside the form and provides depth to the arrangement as well. Gerberas are placed along these lines to create the colorful accent.

My idea came from thinking about the relationship between ikebana and containers in general. The container is functional (it holds water and provides support) and a very important aspect of ikebana design. We try to produce harmony between the materials and container as part of the overall design concept.

However, in this arrangement I experimented to try and blur the boundary between the containers and the materials by attempting to bring them together as closely as possible, both physically and functionally. Three small containers sit inside the ikebana form. Surrounded by the materials, rather than the other way around, the containers themselves become one of the volume elements.

Materials:

Gerbera

Horsetail

Container: Three small containers

chapter four

20 Step-by-Step Arrangements

The following section shows some of my basic arrangements accompanied by step-by-step instructions specifying how each arrangement was made and the types of techniques and designs that I used. I tried to use common materials that could be easily found at your local flower shop and containers of simple design that may be similar to something you already own or that you could readily purchase.

Occasionally, I need to spend extra time making my arrangement because I'm having problems with technique or cannot achieve the form I would like. On other occasions I'll spend less time making my arrangement because everything works well. However, to me the process of making ikebana is more exciting than appreciating the finished piece. Please enjoy the process of making ikebana!

When you complete the ikebana form, try and look at the whole arrangement from a distance (please step back a few steps) to make sure that you have the form that you'd like or to see whether you should change something. When you see the work from a distance, you will observe the proportion, balance, size, form, and color more clearly. I always try to look at my finished work from a distance after cleaning up around the arrangement, so that I can see it clearly without any obstacles. If I find something that needs changing, I'll try a few different adjustments until I attain the form that I like.

Natural-Line Arrangement

The use of lines is one of the most attractive elements in ikebana design. Natural lines are used in this arrangement. When you use the natural line, you need to consider the thickness and shape of the lines. If you're using only one line, select a thick and strong line. If you're using more than one line, select the thicker line as the main line and construct your other lines in tandem with the main line.

Materials:

Curly willow

Aspidistra

Sunflower

Container: Black square container

Mechanics: Kenzan (2)

Technique :
Trimming Branches

When working with branches, I recommend trimming away excess branches in order to make a clean line. Keep excess branches to use as additional lines.

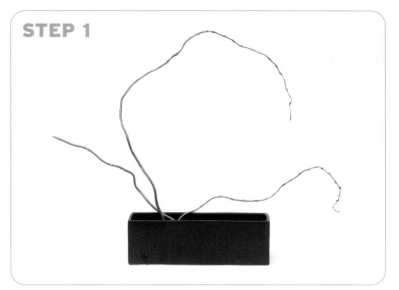

Line Construction

Three natural lines of curly willow are used as the line construction. The longest and sturdiest line is used for the main line. Two other lines are added on both sides of the main line. Select the direction of your lines carefully so that all of the lines achieve harmony with each other.

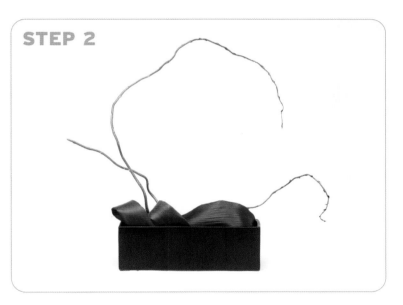

Volume Construction

Next, bend the aspidistra leaves into a curved shape to add volume to the line construction. I use one wide leaf and two thinner leaves to lend rhythm to the arrangement. The thinner leaves are simply two halves of one wide leaf.

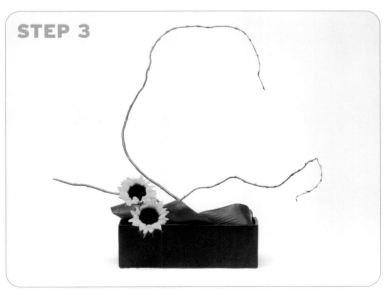

Accent Construction

Finally, two sunflowers are used as the accent. Since the flowers are somewhat big, I cut them short and arranged them low to give the bottom of the form more visual weight and create a stable look.

The finished arrangement.

Curved-Line Arrangement

Looped lines of grass are used in this arrangement. The looping technique draws focus to the curved line form of the grass.

Materials:

Steel grass

Solidago

Iris

Container: black round container

Mechanics: Kenzan (2)

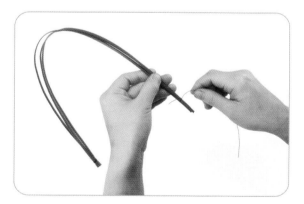

Technique 1: Binding grass

A single strand of grass is too thin to be fixed onto the kenzan without increasing its thickness. I tie a few strands of grass together to make a loop and coil this with green florist wire on both ends. (The steel grass looks like bear grass, but steel grass is more sharp and strong. Please be careful not to cut yourself if making the loops out of steel grass!)

Technique 2: Binding solidago

Solidagos are also too thin to be fixed to the kenzan. I'll bind a few stems of solidagos together using green florist wire. This way the flowers will stick to the kenzan and at the same time will provide thicker volume.

STEP 1

Line Construction

Begin by placing your two kenzans inside of the container, one on the left side and one on the right. Form the grass into curved lines and insert onto the kenzans as shown. (See technique on page 70.) The contrast between the large and the small loops generates rhythmical movement in the form.

STEP 2

Volume Construction

Add the yellow solidago flowers to provide volume to the curved lines. (See technique on page 70.) When adding the solidago, try to hide the kenzan used as the mechanics inside the container.

STEP 3

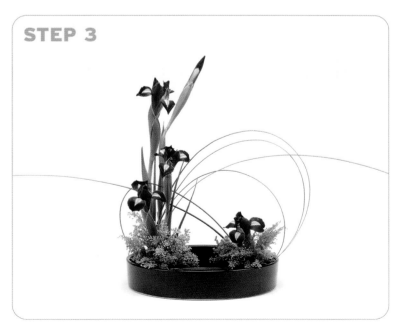

Accent Construction

Place the irises on the kenzans to provide the accent and finish the arrangement. The varied heights of the irises create a livelier looking form in much the same way as the different sized grass loops.

The finished arrangement.

Vertical-Line Arrangement

This is a very simple vertical-line arrangement using only two kinds of materials. A straight-line arrangement gives a more static impression, but makes the site where it is displayed calm and peaceful looking. When using a clear glass container, you need to think about the inside of the glass as part of the design. In this arrangement, lines of horsetail and red anthurium and some stones used inside the glass container become part of the design.

Materials:

Horsetail

Anthurium (red and green)

Container: Two glass
square containers
containing stones

Mechanics: Kenzan (1–2)

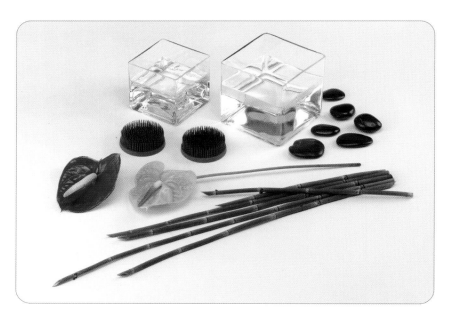

Technique: Using the kenzan

In this arrangement, the kenzan serves as the mechanics for the vertical lines in the thick glass container. (I don't recommend using the kenzan in a thin glass container because the glass can be damaged.) Place stones or similar materials inside the glass container to hide the kenzan.

STEP 1

STEP 2

Line Construction

Place a kenzan in each container* and surround them with your stones (see technique on page 72). Create vertical lines using the horsetails. Tie the horsetails together with florist's wire so that they stand straight up on the kenzan. Later we'll hide the wire itself using one of the anthuriums.

*NOTE: One kenzan must be used to support the horsetail, but a second kenzan may not be needed if the other container will support the red anthurium without using a kenzan.

Accent Construction

Add the red and green anthuriums for the accent. Anthurium is one of the flowers with distinctive features and colors, so every time I use an anthurium, I position it a few different ways to try and find the perspective which best fits the arrangement.

The finished arrangement.

Horizontal-Line Arrangement

The horizontal lines are used for the main line construction in this arrangement. In the same manner that the vertical lines create a static impression, the horizontal lines have a calming effect. However, in this arrangement the group of thick loops is used for volume. The combination of the straight lines and the curved volume creates both calmness and movement in one arrangement.

Materials:

Limonium

Marguerite daisy

Aspidistra

Container: White vase

Mechanics: 16-gauge wire

Technique:

Making a loop using foliage

This is one simple method to make a loop using foliage: Make a small split in one end of the foliage, and insert the other end through it.

STEP 1

Line Construction

The first step is to fit the wire inside the vase (see the "wire support" section on page 24). Then, place the limonium horizontally to create the line element. (Limonium is normally used to add volume to arrangements because of its puffy shape.)

STEP 2

Volume Construction

The second step is to make the looped lines of aspidistra leaves to create the volume (see technique on page 74). Placing them together adds significant depth to the form.

STEP 3

Accent Construction

Finally, the marguerite daisy is used for the accent. The daisy is a very delicate-looking flower, and in this example it is the same color as the vase. In order to craft a distinguished accent amid the thick line and volume, I placed the daisies as a group instead of scattering them.

The finished arrangement.

Geometric-Line Arrangement
Triangular Lines

This arrangement was made with triangular lines. Simply overlapping the small triangles creates depth in the form. This type of geometric design can be matched with numerous sites owing to its simplicity. You may easily change the size of the arrangement by adjusting the number of containers used.

Materials:

Horsetail

Carnation

Container: Two square glass containers containing clear marbles

Technique:

Making a triangular line out of horsetail

This is how I make a triangular line out of horsetail: Cut one end of the stem diagonally, bend the stem into a triangular shape, and then insert one end of the stem into the other end. The diagonal cut will make the ends fit together more easily.

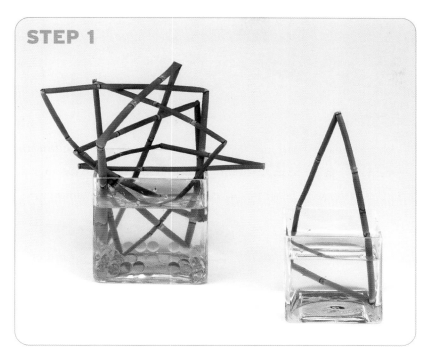

Line Construction

Make the triangular lines out of horsetail. The overlapped triangles used in the larger container add depth to the form. Only one triangle is used in the smaller container to provide contrast with the larger container. Once the first (main) triangular line is fitted firmly inside of the container, the other lines can be added easily.

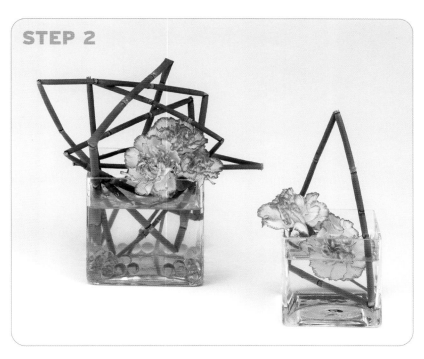

Accent Construction

Use the carnations for the accent. I purposely cut the carnations' stems short in order to show the triangular lines clearly.

The finished arrangement.

Manipulated-Line Arrangement

The folded paper seen in Japanese origami inspired the folded leaves in this arrangement. I could have used numerous different leaves for the folding design, but I choose hala leaves for their flexibility and capacity to form different shapes. You may use a full hala leaf, or only half a leaf by splitting it down the middle. Using different sizes and widths of leaves makes for a more interesting looking form.

Materials:

Hala leaves

Yarrow

Liatris

Container: Tall green vase

Mechanics: 16-gauge wire

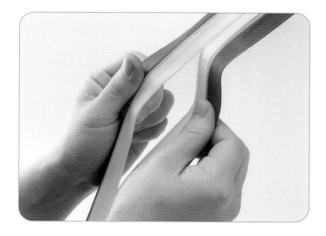

Technique 1:
Splitting hala leaves

Hala leaves are split easily by pulling them apart from the center.

Technique 2:
Folding a hala leaf

This is how I fold a hala leaf—it's just like folding paper.

Line Construction

Place the wire inside of the container (see "Wire Support" page 24). Fold the leaves to create the line element (see the techniques on page 78.) I think that the strong line construction works better visually for this large, tall vase.

Volume Construction

Add the yarrow flowers to form the volume between the lines of hala leaves. Since the folded hala is rather flat, I arrange the yarrows continuously from front to back in order to create more depth.

Accent Construction

Finally, insert the liatris for the color accent. The line and volume constructions are rather short and dense, so I use a tall pointed flower like the liatris as an accent to bring open space (air) into the arrangement.

The finished arrangement.

Sequential Vases

Sequencing arrangements utilize multiple containers to provide added complexity of form. Create a relationship between one container and the others in terms of color and shape. This can be accomplished by using similar colors or designs in the arrangements or similar containers. In this arrangement, I chose containers with the same design and used three of them since the containers were so small.

Materials:

Myrtle

Aster

Container: Three small containers

**Technique 1:
Removing leaves
from the branches**

This shows how I remove leaves from the branches. The visual effect of the form will vary, becoming lighter or heavier looking depending on how many leaves are removed from the branches.

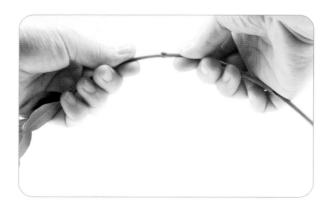

**Technique 2:
Bending the branches**

The soft curved lines of the myrtle branches are made by gently bending them using both hands.

Line Construction

Use the myrtle branches for the line element. I removed most of the leaves from each branch and left only a small section of leaves at the top to help define the unique lines, although this is optional. Gently bend the branches (see the techniques on page 80) so that when placed in the containers the branches will sit almost horizontally and cross from one container to another like bridges. Insert two or three branches per container in this fashion.

Accent Construction

Place a roughly equal amount of asters in each container. The color of the asters serves as an accent, but at the same time their thick shape creates the volume in each container. The thick volume of the asters contrasts nicely with the thin lines.

The finished arrangement.

Glass Container Arrangement

When using a glass container, the first thing I'll do is to remove any foliage from the flower stems that would otherwise sit below the water line. This ensures a clean stem line inside of the vase. There are many types of mechanics that we can use inside a glass container to support the flowers that will also become a part of the design. In this arrangement I use curly willow to support the materials in the container.

Materials:

Chrysanthemum

Aspidistra

Hala leaves

Curly willow

Container: One tall glass container;
one square glass container

Mechanics: Curly willow

Technique:
Preparing the curly willow

Curly willow branches operate as the mechanics to support the materials here. Curly willow is a soft material that is easily bent. Using both hands, scrunch the curly willows together loosely and insert them into the glass container. Because the vase is transparent, the curly willow becomes part of the line element in this arrangement.

STEP 1

Line Construction

Three types of lines—curved, folded, and straight—are used in this one arrangement using two kinds of foliage (hala and aspidistra). Usually, I'll arrange the main line (in this case, the straight line made of hala) first. However, in this arrangement, it is easier to place the bent and folded leaves in the tall container first and to add the additional lines later.

First, insert the curly willow (see the technique on page 82). Then, bend each aspidistra leaf into a softly curved shape, placing three leaves into the tall container and one in the short container.

Next, split the hala leaves into halves. Fold two leaves and place them in the large container. Then, add one straight leaf to each container as shown. A small kenzan can be used in the shorter container should you need further support.

STEP 2

Accent Construction

For the second step, simply add chrysanthemums as the accent. I used the same type of chrysanthemums for the focal point because I believe that the size and shape of this flower is perfectly beautiful by itself and there's no need to mix in other flowers.

The finished arrangement.

Using Floral Tubes for the Mechanics

In this arrangement, floral water tubes are used to keep the flowers fresh. Although the water tube is used mainly in Western-style arrangements, I like using this tool because it allows me to expand my arrangements beyond the limited size of a container. The size of this arrangement can easily be adjusted by cutting the materials (in this case curly willow) shorter or longer than shown here.

Materials:

Gerbera

Curly willow

Yarrow

Purple majesty (ornamental millet)

Mechanics: Floral water tube

Technique 1:
Preparing the curly willow branches

After placing the curly willow branches on the table, cut them diagonally so that the cut sections of the branches are hidden and your arrangement has a more natural look.

Technique 2:
The water tube

This picture shows how the water tube supplies water to the fresh flowers.

STEP 1

Line Construction

The line construction consists of natural lines of curly willow and some straight lines of purple majesty. Cut a quantity of curly willow of sufficient length to fit your display site, and then place the branches horizontally on the site. Trim the thick branches (see the technique on page 84). Place the purple majesties amid the curly willow, inserting them at multiple angles instead of placing them flat. The different angles and the added height will help construct a three-dimensional form. If it is hard to find purple majesty, you can use alternative materials (even some dried leaves or flowers may work well with the color of curly willow).

STEP 2

Volume Construction

Next, add the yellow yarrows as the volume element, using the water tubes as shown on page 84. Create the volume at the center so that it contrasts with the spreading curly willow. This volume also becomes the center point from which the purple majesty stems fan out in different directions.

STEP 3

Accent Construction

Three colorful gerberas mark the focal point to the arrangement as the accent element. Using the water tubes as shown will keep them fresh. Place the gerberas facing different directions along the lines of purple majesty so that the arrangement can be viewed from various directions.
The finished arrangement.

The Basket Container

The basket is often used in Western-style arrangements as a portable container. I also use this kind of basket to bring ikebana arrangements to my friends as gifts. The floral foam keeps the flowers fresh in the basket.

Materials:

Iris

Horsetail

Aster

Liatris

Container: Basket

Mechanics: Floral foam

Technique:
Using asters to cover the floral foam

Asters are used to cover the floral foam in this arrangement. Make sure that your materials completely cover the foam. This is easily accomplished with materials that are puffy or have small flowers attached to one stem.

Tips for Using Floral Foam

Insert the stem of each flower securely into the foam so that each flower can stand freely. Don't use too much pressure, however, because the foam is fairly delicate and will damage easily. Also, be careful to insert the materials into the right place on the foam, because you cannot reuse the same place again for other materials once you make a hole in it. When you've finished the arrangement, look at it from all directions to make sure that the materials fully cover the foam.

STEP 1

Line Construction

The line construction is made of horsetail. The use of both bent and straight lines imparts depth and distinctiveness to the form. Cut your lines shorter to keep the proportion if using a small basket, which also makes it easier to handle for delivery.

To begin, prepare your floral foam (see "Floral Foam" on page 86) and place it in the basket. Next, place the main straight line (the longest) first, and then place the second longest straight line. Bend the other three lines in half as shown and place them along the straight lines. Changing the angles at which you position the bent lines will help give depth to the form.

STEP 2

Volume Construction

Asters are added for thick volume while at the same time they are used to hide the floral foam. Place a group of short asters to create thick volume in the lower area. This will help cover the foam, while allowing the lines of horsetail to be seen clearly.

STEP 3

Accent Construction

Finally, the liatrises and iris are added as the accent element. Even though these flowers have similar violet colors, the pointed features of the liatrises and strong color of the iris create a focal point relative to the other materials. Place one liatris along the straight lines of horsetail to construct a nice balance between the two materials. Place the other flowers at different angles for more depth in the form of the arrangement.

The finished arrangement.

Pruning Design

In this arrangement I pruned the foliage as part of my design. Pruning of excess foliage is necessary if the arrangement is too dense or heavy looking and can also be used to create interesting patterns. It works better if you use larger foliage for this type of design so that you have enough material to create a pattern you like.

Materials:

Tepe leaves

Dendrobium

Container: Two tall white vases

Mechanics: Horizontal supports

Technique 1:
Holding the leaves in place

Left: The large leaves are tied together with green florist's wire so that the leaves are held firmly in place.

Technique 2:
Cutting the foliage to create patterns

Right: This picture shows how I cut excess foliage to create the patterns that I like.

STEP 1

Line Construction

Tepe leaves are used for the line construction in this arrangement. They are well suited for this design because their large bulk makes them easy to prune into the proper shape. Feel free to make any pattern that you like when pruning them. Here, the varied sizes of leaves give the design further complexity.

First, create your horizontal supports (see "Horizontal Supports" on page 22). Prune all or some of the leaves into different sizes or shapes. Then, choose the main line (the longest or widest one) and secondary line in your leaves. Tie the two lines together with florist's wire to support them in the container more securely. Add the other leaves from the front, side, and back to create depth in the form. As you are adding leaves, use florist's wire to tie parts of the leaves together whenever you need additional support.

STEP 2

Accent Construction

I use a group of strongly colored dendrobiums as the accent element. Since the pruned tepe leaves are lighter looking, I placed the strong focal point of dendrobium in only one of the vases to contrast with the line element. A group of flowers also adds volume to the form at the same time.

The finished arrangement.

Stacking Design

T he stacking design is used for this arrangement. The overlapping piling of the materials creates a three-dimensional effect.

Materials:

Galax leaves

Iris

Chrysanthemum (pompon cushion)

Container: Brown basin type

Mechanics: Kenzan (1)

Technique:

Piling up the galax leaves

The stacking design is made simply by piling the galax leaves one on top of the other. This creates the volume in the form and also helps hide the kenzan.

Volume Construction

Stack the galax leaves on top of one another as shown. Note that the first galax leaves used at the bottom of the pile are stacked flat to completely cover the kenzan, while the galax used at the top are stacked at different angles to add volume to the form.

Accent Construction

The complementary colors of the violet irises and yellow chrysanthemums become the accent here. Change the height of the irises and arrange them from front to back and from shortest to tallest to generate a nice movement in the form. Use the larger iris in the lower place and the smaller iris or bud higher up so the form will have visual stability.

Instead of placing the yellow chrysanthemums with the irises on the kenzan, they are used as floating flowers on the surface of the water so that the water becomes part of the design element.

The finished arrangement.

Twisting Design

A twisting design is used in this arrangement. As a result of twisting the leaves, their flat shape becomes a three-dimensional form. Create complicated twisted lines or add just one or two twists, depending on the form you would like. Either way, you'll be sure to help make your arrangement unique.

Materials:

Calla lily

Aspidistra

Container: Tall brown container

Mechanics: Cross-supports

Technique 1:
The cross-support

The cross-support will help secure the materials inside the container.

Technique 2: Twisting leaves

The twisting technique adds an element of movement into flat foliage. Split the center of the leaf down the middle, making sure not to split the leaf in half, then bend the tip back and insert it through the hole you've just made.

Technique 3:
Opening a calla lily's petals

Opening a calla lily's petals will enlarge its appearance and can change its character completely.

STEP 1

Line Construction

Place your cross-supports inside the vase (see the technique on page 92). The twisted aspidistra leaves create the curved line construction. Because the curved lines are used as a group this again adds volume to the form. Choose the largest leaf to use as your main line, twist it into shape (see the technique on page 92), and place it inside the container. Create some more twisted leaves out of your longer leaves, and then place these along the main line. Once a group of long twisted leaves is stabilized inside the container, you can then add additional shorter or thinner lines. Make the form of the lines almost round so that your lines can be seen when viewed from different directions.

STEP 2

Accent Construction

Calla lilies are used as the accent. Add the calla lilies from the center at multiple angles so that they can be viewed from different directions along with your curved lines. Use the larger calla lilies at the lower center area to create a strong focal point and use the smaller ones alongside the longer stems. The twisted lines produce a dense looking form. Adding a few long lines of calla lilies, however, makes the arrangement lighter and less dense.

The finished arrangement.

Shredding Technique

A shredding technique is used for this arrangement. Different effects can be produced, depending on how you shred the leaves or the kinds of leaves you use, but in any case this added touch gives some style to an otherwise ordinary arrangement.

Materials:

Aspidistra

Dendrobium

Container: Two vases

Technique:
Shredding leaves

Shredding gives leaves an airier, lighter appearance. This photo shows how a leaf is shredded. Aspidistra is a thin and soft material that you can shred by hand without difficulty.

STEP 1

Line Construction

Shredded aspidistra leaves are used for the line construction. The leaves are placed to look as if they're floating in the air between the two vases, and the negative space that we can see through the shredded leaves becomes part of the design element.

First shred the leaf. Aspidistra leaves can easily be shredded using your hands (see technique on page 94). Then make your additional stems. Cut some 4-inch to 5-inch stems from your extra aspidistra leaves or other additional materials. Place one stem at the top of each leaf, and tie these together with green florist's wire (see the materials photograph, which shows the leaves with additional stems). Insert the stems on the ends of each leaf into the containers as shown, and position the leaves so that some nice lines are formed between the two containers.

STEP 2

Accent Construction

Given that the shredded leaves create some thin and airy lines, I add a group of dendrobrium as strong focal points for the accent element. Use longer and shorter flowers in each vase because the contrast will enhance your composition.

The finished arrangement.

Tying Design

Tying long foliage such as steel grass, aspidistra, or horsetail into knots or loops is another great technique to bring flair to your arrangements. Here, I make a shorter arrangement that makes a suitable dinner table decoration.

Materials:

Statice

Iris

Steel grass

Container: Basket with two small containers

Mechanics: Kenzan (2)

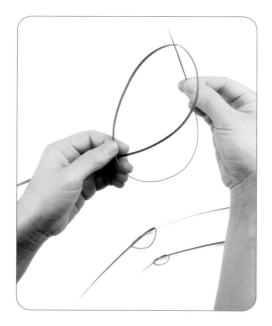

Technique:
Tying long foliage

This is a very simple way of adding an interesting element to the foliage. You can tie the length of foliage just like tying a ribbon.

Volume Construction

I usually start an arrangement by making the line construction. However, in this arrangement, I started to make the form out of volume for my first step because the lines of grass are used for decoration rather than for line construction.

Create the thick volume by placing the statice all over the inside of the basket, as if the statice were blooming in the field. At the same time, try and cover the two kenzans with statice as much as you can.

Accent Construction

To have a nice color contrast against the pink statice, violet irises are added as the accent element. Add the irises from front to back among the statice to give your form depth. I added one longer-stemmed iris bud among the thick flowers, which makes the arrangement much less dense.

Decorative Lines

Make the knotted lines out of long thin leaves (see the technique on page 96). I used steel grass, but you should be careful since this grass is sharp and strong, and you can cut yourself easily. Bear grass can be substituted for steel grass.

Add the knotted lines as the last step to complete the form. With the arrangement's low height and thick volume, adding a few long lines like this makes the arrangement lighter looking. As a result of adding these long lines, the negative space (empty space forming the background of the ikebana) also becomes part of the design element.

The finished arrangement.

Cupped Design

This is another simple way of transforming your natural materials into a more sculpted form. In this arrangement, the flat foliage is turned into a three-dimensional shape similar to a small cup that also mirrors the lilies used here.

Materials:

Calla lily

Galax leaves

Tepe leaves

Container: Basket with a small container

Mechanics: Kenzan (1) (placed in a small plastic container)

Technique:
Making a cupped shape from foliage

To make the cupped shape out of the flat foliage, I simply roll the flat galax leaf into a cupped shape and use green florist's wire to tie the ends of the leaf together.

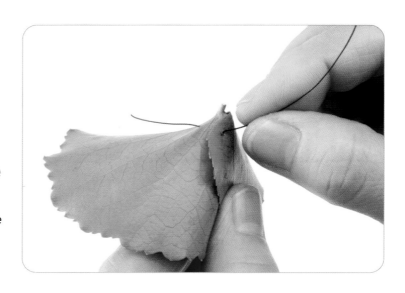

Line Construction

Three tepe leaves are placed both inside and outside of the basket container as the line construction. I wanted to create a continuous line element because of the large mesh, which allows you to see inside the container. So, instead of keeping the inside and outside space separate, I added one of the leaves under the basket to create the extended lines. First, prune the tepe leaves. Then, place them pointing outward from the left and right sides of the container. (The tepe leaf placed under the container is optional).

Volume Construction

Make the cupped galax leaves (see the technique on page 98), and then place these as a group inside the container. The galax leaves are placed as a group so that they contrast with the extended lines and add volume to the form.

Accent Construction

Add a group of calla lilies next to the galax leaves as the accent element. Adding the flowers as a group imparts thicker volume to the form. Because the cupped galax leaves appear similar in shape to the calla lilies, arranging them side by side makes it seem as if some of the leaves were transformed into flowers.

The finished arrangement.

Three Basic Ikebana Techniques

This arrangement utilizes three basic ikebana techniques: bending branches, removing excess leaves from flower stems, and attaching two different kinds of splints to thin stems. Even making a freestyle ikebana arrangement requires knowledge of the basic techniques that allow us to craft our intended form.

Materials:

Pussy willow

Chrysanthemum (yellow pompon button)

Chrysanthemum (violet and yellow pompon cushion)

Container: Square black container

Mechanics: Kenzan (2)

Technique 1: Attaching stem splints

The basic ikebana techniques for attaching stem splints are shown: One half of a thick stem is attached as a splint to the thin chrysanthemum stem. A cap splint is shown also.

Technique 2: Removing excess leaves

Excess leaves are removed from these flowers before making the arrangement.

STEP 1

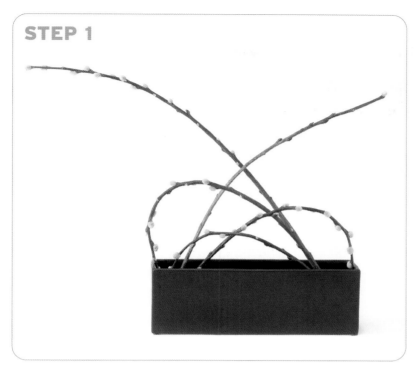

Line Construction

Before you begin, place the two kenzans inside the container, one on the right and the other on the left.

Use the pussy willow to create the line construction. Create the main line using the natural lines of the pussy willow. Then, add another natural line crossing the main line.

Make a few curved lines out of pussy willow, and add these curved lines alongside the natural lines. Because pussy willow is easy to bend, it's a good material with which to practice bending branches.

STEP 2

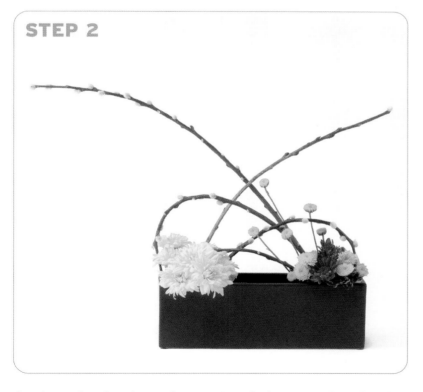

Accent Construction

Three kinds of chrysanthemums are added as the accent. But again, because they are arranged as a group, they act secondarily as a volume element. Even though the same family of flowers is used, the contrast between the yellow and violet flowers marks the focal point of this arrangement. Make sure to arrange all the accents toward the bottom of your arrangement in order to present the lines of pussy willows clearly.

Insert the larger chrysanthemums into the kenzan sitting in the left side of the container first, and then insert the other chrysanthemums into the kenzan on the right side. Finally, add the short and long stemmed chrysanthemums to complete the form.

The finished arrangement.

Rolled Design in a Basin

A rolled foliage design is showcased in a basin style container in this arrangement. The flat leaves of aspidistra are rolled into a tubular shape, giving the flat leaves an unexpected sculptural form. This arrangement was designed to be viewed from above and is suited for display on a low table.

Materials:

Calla lily

Statice

Steel grass

Aspidistra

Container: Brown basin type containing stones

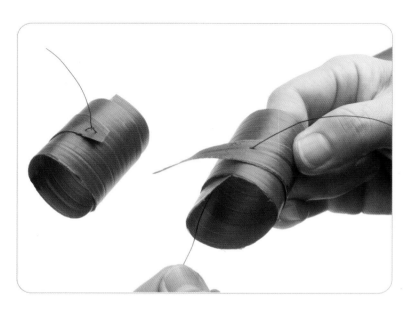

Technique:
Making rolled leaves

This is how I make the rolled leaves. Many types of flat leaves will work fine for this technique, although I use aspidistra leaves in this arrangement. First, cut the aspidistra into different widths. Next, simply roll it and tie the end of each leaf with green florist's wire.

STEP 1

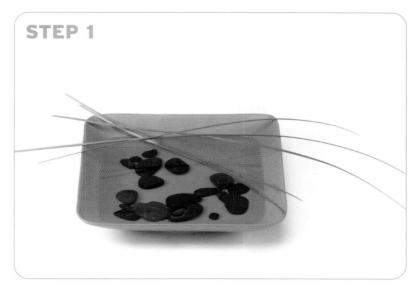

STEP 2

STEP 3

Line Construction

Lay the steel grass naturally across the lip of the basin, but fan out the ends of each blade to keep your lines distinct. For a more interesting look, use long and short blades of grass together rather than keeping them an even length. Small stones are used at the bottom of the container as a decoration and to convey the look of a pond.

Volume Construction

Aspidistra leaves are rolled and placed as a group to add volume to the arrangement. In order to vary the size of your rolled leaves, first cut the aspidistra into different widths. Then, roll each of the leaves into a small tubular form (see the technique on page 102). Place the leaves inside of the basin, leaving some space in between them so you can see some of the stones on the bottom.

Accent Construction

Pink statice and calla lilies are added as the accent element. Cut the statice and calla lilies short so they can be fit into the small rolled-up leaves. Use the calla lilies for the main accent and place them inside of the rolled leaves at the center. Then, place the statice into the remaining rolled leaves surrounding the calla lilies. The finished arrangement.

Using Artificial Materials

Wire is a material ordinarily used inside of the container to support the flower stems, but I think that some kinds of wire have an interesting texture that make them desirable for use as part of the container itself. For this arrangement, I made a box-shaped container out of flat wire and placed two glass containers inside.

Materials:

Pussy willow

Chrysanthemum (yellow pompon button)

Baby's breath

Hypericum

Container: Two square glass containers
and box-shaped wire

Technique:

Inserting the pussy willow

This is how the pussy willows are inserted through the box-shaped wire mesh. The pussy willows are thin, flexible materials, so they're easy to insert through the wire mesh.

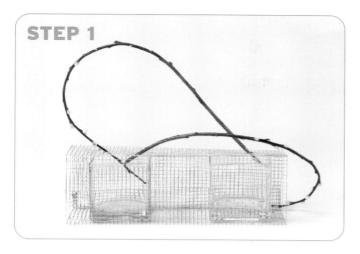

Line Construction

Curved pussy willow is used as the line element and inserted through the wire mesh to give it support. Pussy willow is a rather thin material, so select your sturdiest branch, with a strong line, as your main line. Cut the branch and bend it into a curved shape, then insert it through the wire mesh to make the larger line first.

Cut another sturdy line and bend it into a curved shape. Insert this branch through the wire mesh to make the smaller curved line. When inserting these lines through the wire mesh, insert them from multiple angles (from front to back along the top, for example, or from the side to the top), instead of making a totally flat curved line. Lines inserted at different angles create depth and movement in the form.

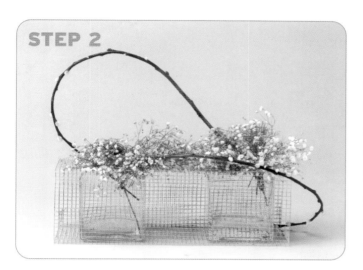

Volume Construction

Baby's breath is used to add thick volume that stands out nicely against the two lines. Cut the baby's breath short and remove the excess leaves from the stems. Insert the stems through the wire mesh and into the glass container so that they touch the water. If the mesh is big enough, you can tie a few stems of baby's breath together and insert them as a group through the wire mesh. (This is an easy way to thicken the volume.)

Accent Construction

Yellow pompon buttons and hypericum are added as the accent to finish the arrangement. Even though these flowers are rather small, the combination of two primary colors (red and yellow) becomes a strong focal point.

Cut the accent flowers short and insert them through the wire mesh into the glass containers. Place an approximately equal amount of red and yellow flowers in each container, because having an even combination of these two colors creates stronger focal points than letting one color predominate. The finished arrangement.

Floating Flowers in a Basin

This arrangement uses a floating flower design in which the water inside of the container becomes one of the design elements. This arrangement is also best viewed from a higher vantage point and can be displayed on a coffee table or low counter.

Materials:

Steel grass

Dendrobium

Container: Shallow round black container

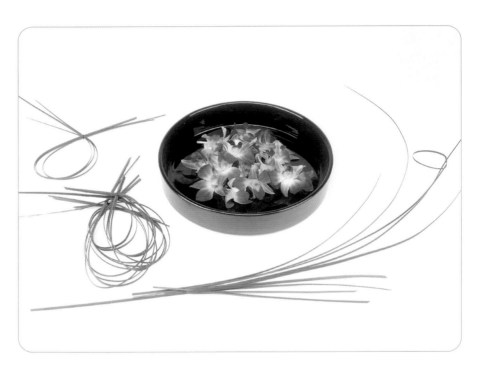

Technique:
Making a loop

This is how a loop is made. We can make the loop out of any long grass such as bear grass or steel grass. I'll often make a loop out of several strands of grass and then cut both ends to keep it clean looking. Tie each loop with a piece of green floral wire. Use more or fewer strands of grass to adjust the size of the loop.

STEP 1

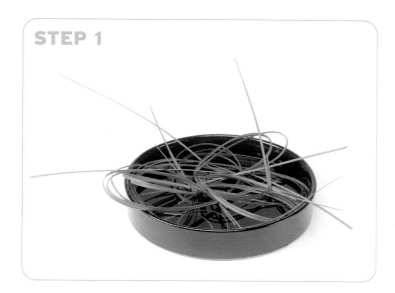

Line Construction

Looped lines of steel grass are placed inside the container. Overlapping the lines creates a more intricate-looking line element.

The first step is making the looped lines (see the technique on page 106). Make big, medium, and small loops and place them inside of the container at overlapping angles relative to one another.

STEP 2

Accent Construction

The dendrobium contrasts with the dark color of the container as the accent element. Because thin lines are used for the line element, I placed the dendrobiums as a group to balance the composition and add volume.

Dendrobium flowers grow in clusters along a large stem. Gently pull individual flowers from the main stem and place them one by one in a group upon the grass. I placed them somewhat off-center to allow the water inside the container to show through as part of the design element.

The finished arrangement.

Glossary

The following are some ikebana related Japanese terms often referred to in ikebana classes and many of which I reference elsewhere in this book.

Chabana: A style of ikebana. The *chabana*, or "tea flower," is most often arranged in the tea-room where a tea ceremony is held.

Hanabasami: We call flower scissors *hanabasami* in Japanese. The ikebana scissors are one of the basic tools used for creating ikebana, and a good pair helps us to make the ikebana form smoothly. I have been using the same pair of ikebana scissors for a long time.

Ikebana: *Ike* means "life", while *hana* or *bana* means "flowers." *Ikebana* may be literally translated as "living flowers," but we can find a deeper meaning as well. When we make ikebana, the flowers are given new life in the container after they are cut from the soil. Ikebana then can also mean "to bring life to the flowers."

Kabin: A vase-style container. It is used for the nageire style of arrangement.

Kado: *Ka* means "flower" and *do* means "way." *Kado*, therefore, literally translated means "the way of flowers" (or, more accurately, "the way of mastering flower arrangement"). By the word *do*, or way, we mean the way in which we master the art form. Many artists who have mastered Ikebana or other traditional Japanese arts such as the tea ceremony have continually refined their expertise over many years.

Kago: A basket container. It is generally used for summertime arrangements.

Kaki: The Japanese term for a container used for Ikebana.

Kenzan: An ikebana tool. The kenzan is used for the moribana style arrangement to support materials inside of the container. The kenzan is also referred to as an English needlepoint holder or a "frog."

Mizukiri: Water absorption. *Mizukiri* means "to cut the stem underwater." This is the standard technique used to keep flowers fresh longer and works for many types of flowers.

Moribana: A piled-up style of ikebana arranged in a shallow container.

Nageire: A style of ikebana, *Nageire* means "to throw into" in Japanese. The *kabin*, or upright style container, is used for this type of arrangement.

Suiban: A basin-style container. It is a relatively shallow container similar to a flat bowl.

Tokonoma: The "tokonoma" is the alcove, or recessed area, in a traditional Japanese home. Ikebana is often arranged in the tokonoma along with other artworks.

Resources

Recommended Reading

Howze, Allan and James Moretz. *Nature into Art: Designing with Our Planet*. Chicago:
Flowerian Publishers, 1999.
This book illustrates various styles of western floral design with gorgeous photos. It provides instruction in using color and shape for different styles and explains other design fundamentals. I was very impressed by the inventive contemporary works and various techniques shown in this book.

Intakul, Sakul and Wongvipa Devahastin na Ayudhya. *Tropical Colors: The Art of Living with Tropical Flowers*. Singapore: Periplus Editions, 2003.
This book is one of the most beautiful floral design books that I have ever come across. The harmony between the flowers and the beautiful sites is quite remarkable.

Lefferts, Vena with John Kelsey. *Floral Style: The Art of Arranging Flowers*. New York: Hugh Lauter Levin Associates, Inc., 1996.
This book serves primarily as an introduction to western floral design, but also discusses Ikebana-style arrangements. It explains all the basic floral design styles, tools and supplies, containers, design fundamentals, and much more.

Sato, Shozo. *The Art of Arranging Flowers: A Complete Guide to Japanese Ikebana*. New York: Harry N. Abrams, Inc., 1965.
I found this book at the local library in Chicago. It is practically an Ikebana encyclopedia, providing a detailed history of ikebana as well as numerous photos and explanations of different Ikabana styles, equipment, techniques, etc.

Stark, David and Avi Adler. *Wild Flowers*. New York: Clarkson Potter, 2003.
The arrangements in this work are particularly impressive to me because they appear more like installation art works than typical floral designs. You should enjoy their creative approach and the interesting use of color.

These are some online stores that I came across which offer different kinds of ikebana tools and supplies, including various containers and other ikebana books.

www.japanese-gardening.com
(ikebana, bonsai, and Japanese gardening supplies)

www.stonelantern.com
(ikebana books, containers, and ikebana tools such as kenzans)

www.save-on-crafts.com
(both ikebana-style and Western-style tools and supplies such as floral foam)

www.samadhi-japanese-arts.com
(ikebana supplies and tools)

www.holymtn.com
(ikebana containers, tools, and supplies)

www.chopa.com
(ikebana books, containers, and tools)

In this book, I introduce my method of freestyle ikebana arranging that is influenced by Western style arrangements and my art background. If you are interested in learning more about ikebana, I recommend that you take ikebana classes and also try to attend an ikebana demonstration or exhibition.

There are so many ikebana schools and each have their own curriculum. Since Ikebana has become more recognized internationally, many of the Japanese schools also offer classes overseas. The following are some major ikebana schools and organizations.

Ikenobo School

The Ikenobo School is recognized as the originator of ikebana and has the longest history.
www.ikenobo.jp/english/

Ohara School

This school was founded in the late 19th Century. The Moribana style was created by the Ohara school.
www.ohararyu.or.jp/english/ikebana/ohararyu.htm

Sogetsu School

This school was founded in the early 20th Century. They are known for creating modern and contemporary styles of ikebana.
www.sogetsu.or.jp/english/ikebana/index.html

Ikebana International

A worldwide organization with a beautiful web site that tells you about their activities, including ikebana events, exhibitions and information about different ikebana schools.
www.ikebanahq.org

Index

accent, 29
  design element, 35–36
  moribana style, 45–48
  nagiere style, 48–51
  see also individual arrangements
allium, 56–57
altar, 2
anthurium, 59, 72
architecture
  contemporary influence of, 5–6
  traditional influence of, 3
artificial materials, 38, 41, 57, 104
aspidistra, 34–35, 38
  gallery arrangements, 58, 60, 63
  step-by-step arrangements, 68, 74, 82, 92, 94, 102
aster, 80, 86
aster matsumoto, 12, 49–51
asymmetrical form, 4, 39–41, 50

baby's breath, 48–50, 56, 59, 104
balance, 29, 39–41
buddha, 2
buddhism, 2
branches, 17–19, 68, 80

calla lily, 61, 92, 98, 102
caps, 20
carnation, 26, 64, 76
chabana style, 4
chrysanthemum, 51, 82, 90, 100, 104
color, 10, 35–36, 43, 63
commercial arrangements, 2
containers, 9–12, 25, 44
  see also individual arrangements
contemporary style, 4–7
craspedia, 12, 58

curly willow, 31–34, 64
  as mechanics, 82
  cutting, 84
  step-by-step arrangements, 68, 82, 84
cutting, 18

dahlia, 60
daisy, 74
dendrobium, 62, 88, 94, 106
density, 43
depth, 29, 34–35
display site, 5–6
  choosing, 44
  relationship to container, 10
  viewer perspective of, 25–26

floral foam, 15, 27, 86
foliage, 60, 74, 88, 96, 98
  see also leaves
freestyle ikebana, 7, 53–54

galax leaves, 26, 62, 90, 98
gerbera, 63, 65, 84

hala leaves, 59, 78, 82
horestail, 30
  gallery arrangements 63, 65
  moribana style, 45
  step-by-step arrangements, 72, 76, 86
hypericum, 63, 104

iris, 70, 86, 90, 96

kado, 1
kenzan, 4
  binding materials for, 70
  glass container, 72

moribana style 45–48
    shallow container, 90
    techniques using, 19–22
    see also individual arrangements

leaves
    cleaning, 17
    removing excess 80, 100
    rolled, 102
    shredding, 54, 94
    splitting and folding, 78
    twisting, 92
    see also foliage
liatris, 78, 86
limonium, 74
lines
    design element, 29–34
    moribana style, 45–48
    nageire style, 48–51
    symbolism of, 1
    see also individual arrangements

marbles, 15
mass, 34–35
mechanics, 14–15, 18–24, 82, 84
    see also individual arrangements
minimalism, 7, 30, 57
mizukiri. see water absorption
moribana style, 3–5, 9, 45–48
myrtle branches 49-50, 80

nageire style, 4, 9, 48–51
noncommercial arrangements, 2

offerings, 2
ornamental millet. see purple majesty

pompom cushion, 90, 100, 104
    see also chrysanthemum
positive and negative space, 29, 42
purple majesty (ornamental millet), 64, 84
pussy willow, 100, 104
queen anne's lace, 61

rikka style, 3–4

rokkakudo temple, 2
roses, 45–47, 58

sado, 1
scissors, 13
shape, 29, 37–38, 43
shodo, 1
solidago, 45, 58, 70
space, 29
splints, 21, 100
statice, 96, 102
steel grass
    gallery arrangements, 56, 60–62
    step-by-step arrangements, 70, 96, 102, 106
stones, 14
sunflower, 58, 68
supports, 22–24, 48–51
symmetrical form, 40–41, 48–50, 59, 62, 64

tea ceremony, 1, 4
techniques, 16–24
tepe, 34, 88, 98
texture, 43, 104
tokonoma (alcove), 2–3, 5
tools, 9, 13–15
tree fern, 35, 62

volume, 29
    as design element, 34–35
    in moribana style, 45–48
    in nageire style, 48–51
    see also individual arrangements

water absorption (mizukiri), 16, 25
water tubes, 15, 84
wire, 14, 21–22, 24

yarrow, 78, 84

About the Author

Growing up in Japan, Keiko Kubo studied ikebana like many other Japanese women and started taking classes with her mother as a teenager. Keiko's mother, who always encouraged her art training, told Keiko that if she knew how to arrange flowers she could create her art anywhere in the world—all she would really need were a pair of scissors and her imagination.

Keiko came to the United States to pursue her studies in art after graduating from college and obtaining her teaching license for ikebana. She graduated from the School of the Art Institute of Chicago with a master of fine arts degree in Studio, majoring in sculpture, and has additionally studied Western floral art.

Keiko resides in Chicago, Illinois, where she is working toward opening her own floral design studio. If you have any questions or comments for Keiko, she may be reached at keiko@ikebanabykeiko.com.

About the Photographer

Erich Schrempp is a Chicago-based photographer specializing in illustrative images. His fine art and commissioned work can be viewed at www.schremppstudio.com.